Moments For Mindset
Curtis Ingersoll

ISBN 979-8-89569-138-0

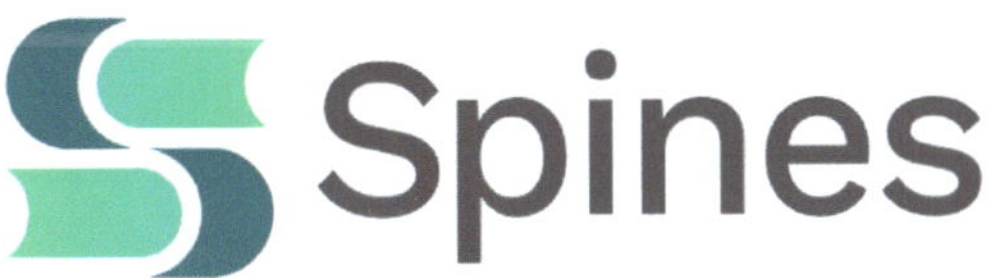

Moments For Mindset

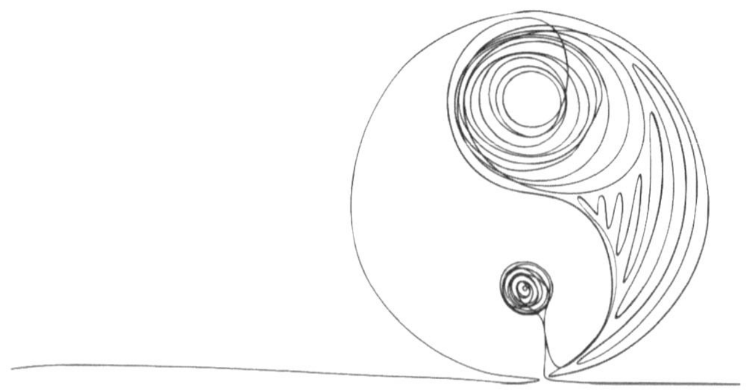

Moments For Mindset

A Journey to Now

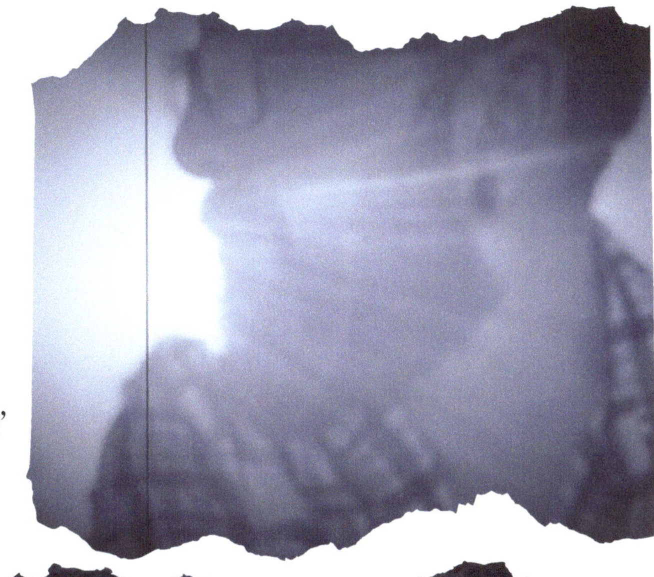

Photography: by Lexi Re'
& Curtis Ingersoll

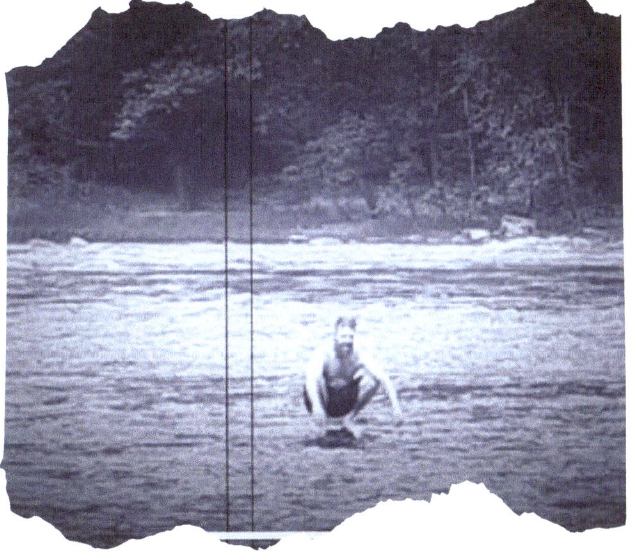

Intro by AI

Compendium Media : Florida

Introduction

In the sun-drenched landscapes of South Florida, amidst the vibrant tapestry of the late 80s, a journey of resilience and self-discovery began for a child born to a set scared teenagers at 8:11 am on 10/11, 1987. Growing up against the backdrop of adversity, this individual's early years were marked by the complexities of navigating life's challenges solo. Yet, within the crucible of hardship, seeds of resilience were sown, laying the foundation for an extraordinary voyage.

As adolescence unfolded, an insatiable curiosity emerged, leading to a deep exploration of metaphysical concepts. Amidst the swaying palms and azure skies, this seeker delved into the mysteries of existence, finding solace and illumination within the realms of metaphysics. These studies became not only a sanctuary but also a beacon of hope amidst the tumultuous seas of mental health struggles.

In the quiet hours of introspection, amidst the whispers of the Florida breeze, writing became a refuge—a means to untangle the threads of thoughts and emotions woven within. Through the alchemy of pen and paper, the tumult of the mind found expression, giving birth to narratives that mirrored the complexities of the human experience.

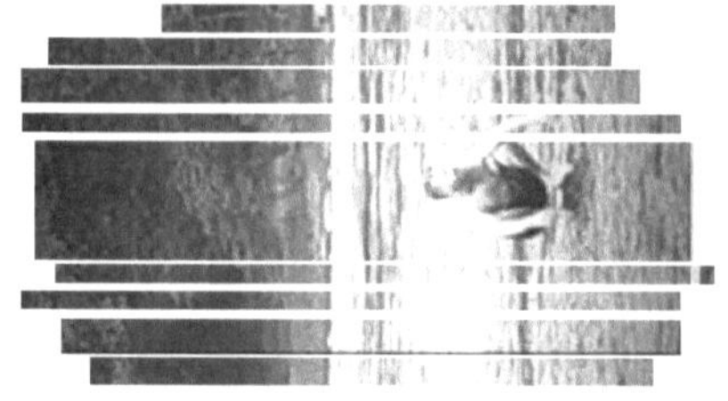

Yet, it was within the stillness of meditation that the true depths of understanding were plumbed. Amidst the chaos of the external world, this individual found sanctuary in the silence within, discovering a profound connection to the essence of being.

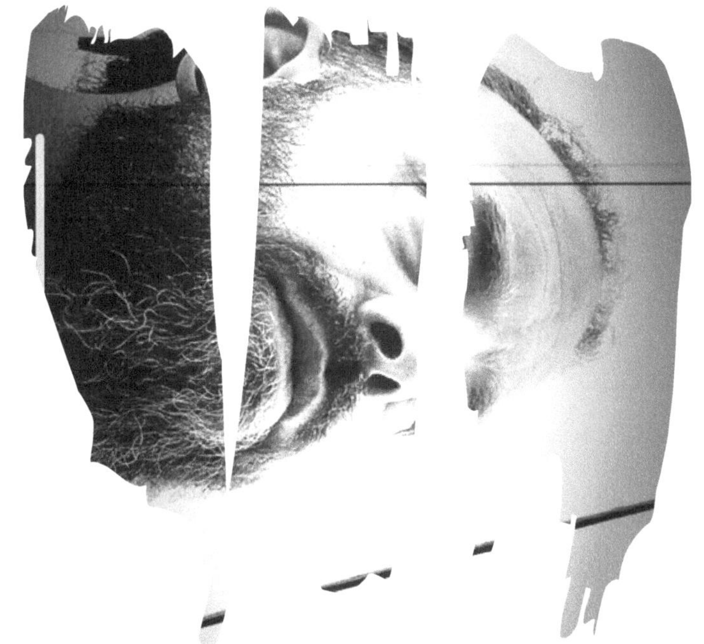

Now, as the pages of this book unfold, the author invites you on a to take a moment for yourself — a journey woven with aesthetic of vulnerability through poetry, photography, and creative theories. As the purpose is for a stand alone meditative moments and writings that are conducive to peace. Through the lens of personal experience, they offer insights into a somewhat comedic but deep approach to time. Join us for a moment as we facilitate a little love in the ways we know how.

In the Moment

Contents *of* Time

A moment in Time

A lot of what I share in this book is from my own experience, my personal study , and non certified non licensed opinion. However a lot of what I have studied can be looked up some will have references for what I focus on. This is some of my thoughts , opinions , theories , writings , photography , poems and little bits of me in a fun stand alone meditative experience. The point this book and the series around it is learning what moment is best to take for you when you need a little rest and reprieve.

These are things that have helped me along the way

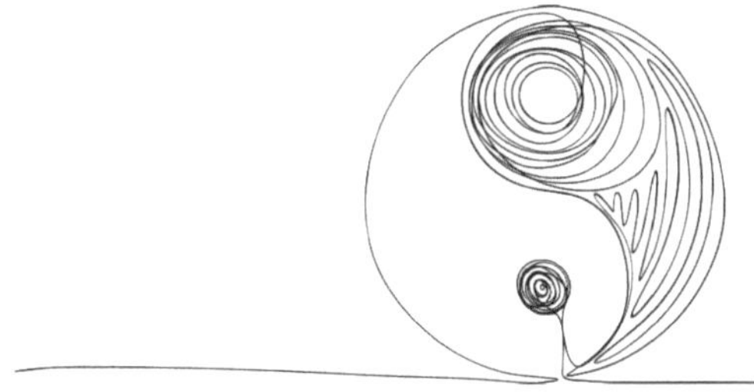

Time is summed up An a blink The second hand A thought of a breath A shadow of the sun A grain of sand falling A flash of lightening A jolt of the nerves A hug A kiss The period at the end of this sentence.

A faculty of moments

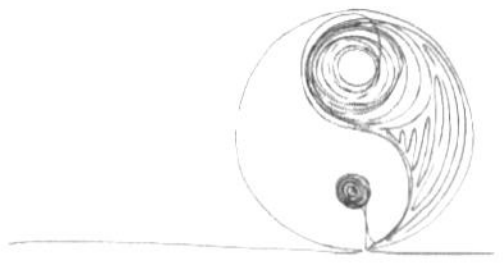

time could be money to some time could be effort to others time could be rest and peace time can be excited chaos time can be family time can be nature time can be slept time can be death

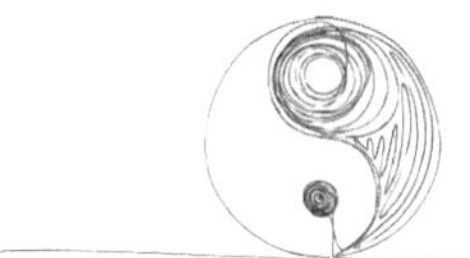

Many famous quotes , poems , and various forms of art depict time in some much unique essence. Music and art directed by the hands have a very individual "time stamp" to it. There is a quote that portrays that title best for me

"Art is how we decorate space, music is how we decorate time"

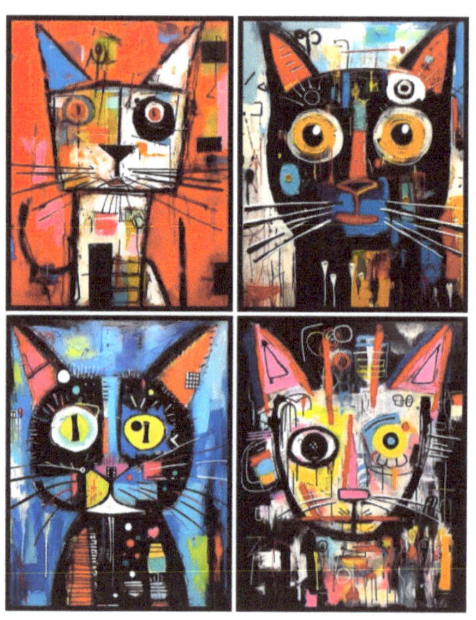

by Jean-Michel Basquiat
A New York painter

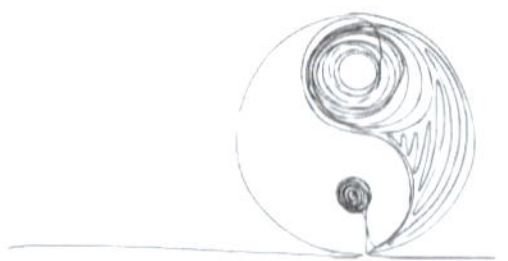

A great reminder of time is our bodies.
A glance in the mirror can be shocking
The feeling when your now
The old-timer
“Back in my day mirrors were better” “Back in my day we didn't have time” "Back in my day it was night" “Back in my day if you wanted to call some one you took a real deep breath and yelled ” “When I was your age boy, I told the clock what time it was”

Where did the all the time go?

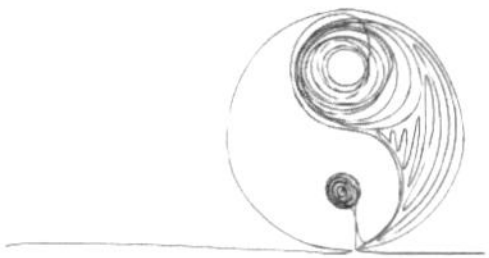

Time has been time. Its something that
is applied but not tangible as a blanket across
our minds and the cosmos. Looking into the philosophy
about time it appears that a second and a moment
are different things to me. A moment is like a second
that is stretched for its observer.
When two lovers lean in to kiss for the first time,
the heart is what adds significance to it.
If a person is hesitant its noticeable ,
but if the moment is meaningful then
the hands slowly embrace the cheek , as the eyelids
slowly shut , that moment of vulnerability and the
nerves around it could feel like an eternity.
The heart and an open mind is a key
to Now.

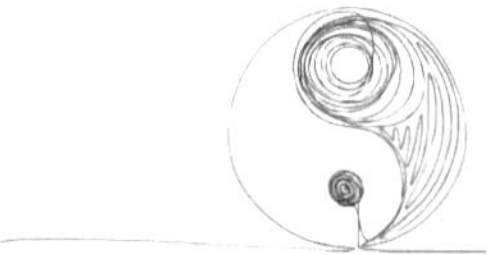

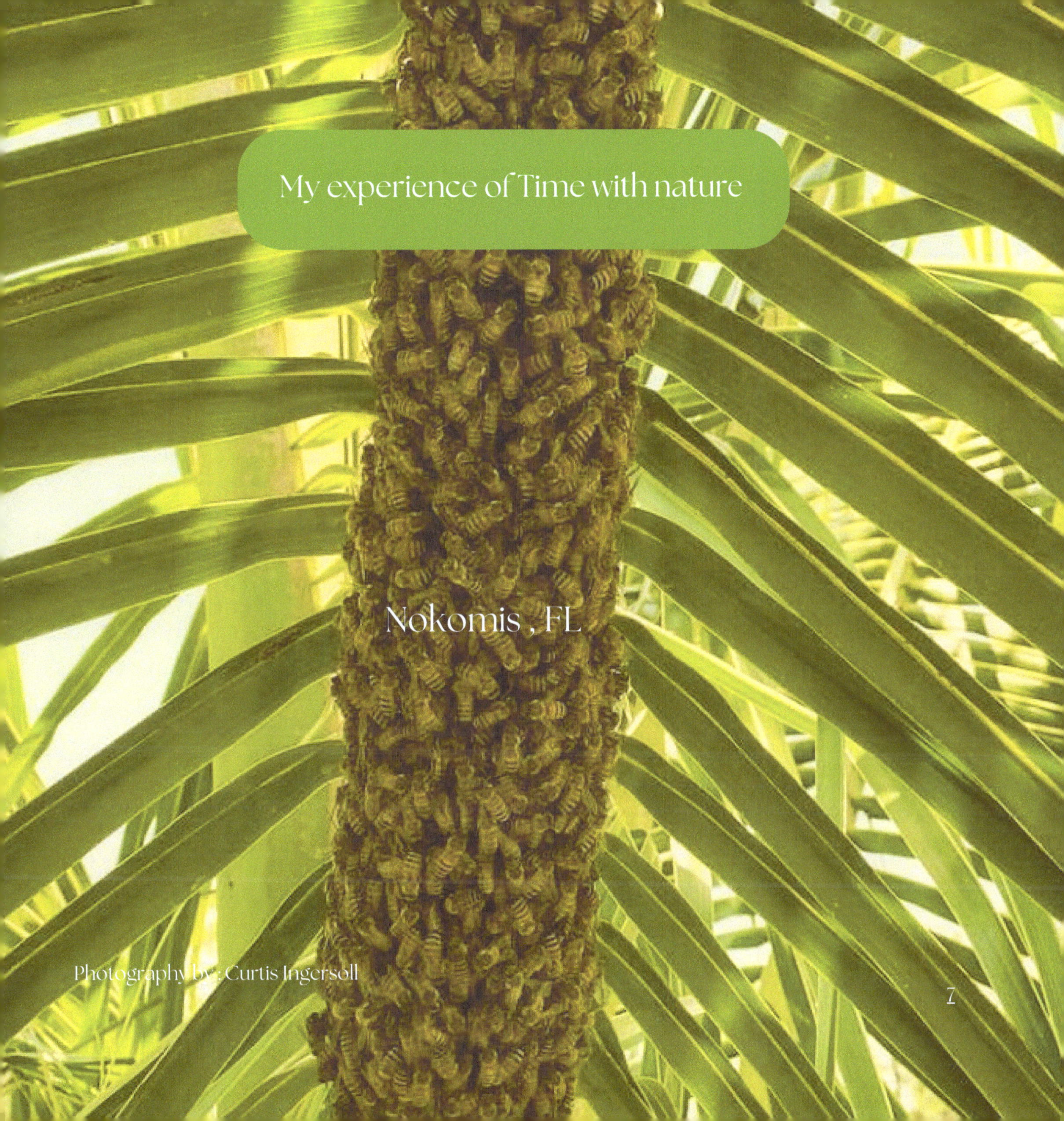
My experience of Time with nature
Nokomis , FL
Photography by : Curtis Ingersoll

The stillness. The flow. Inner peace.
All of these aspects can be achieved simply by getting back into nature. Sitting in stillness, watching the leaves blow in the wind as the hairs tickle your sunburnt neck.

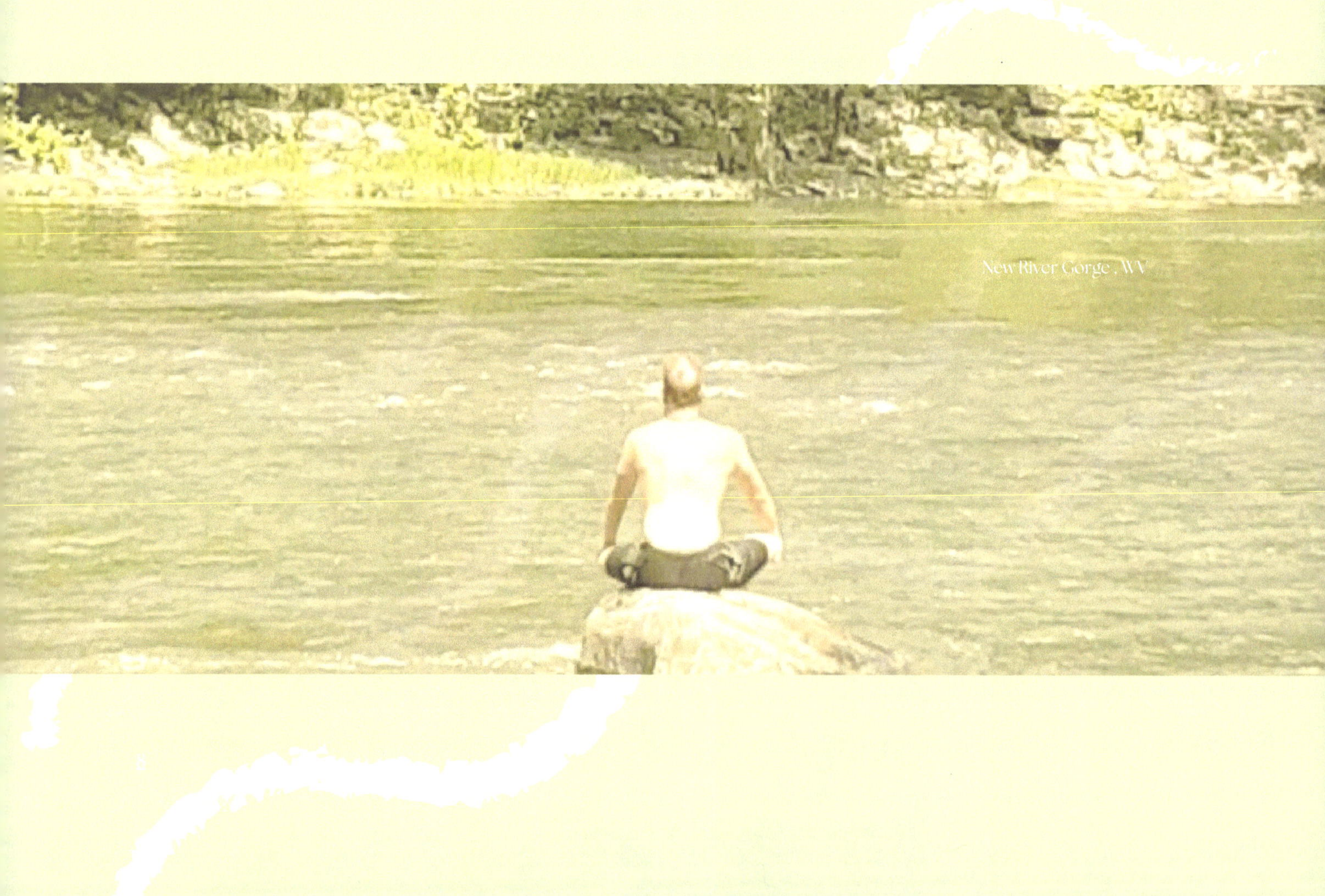
New River Gorge, WV

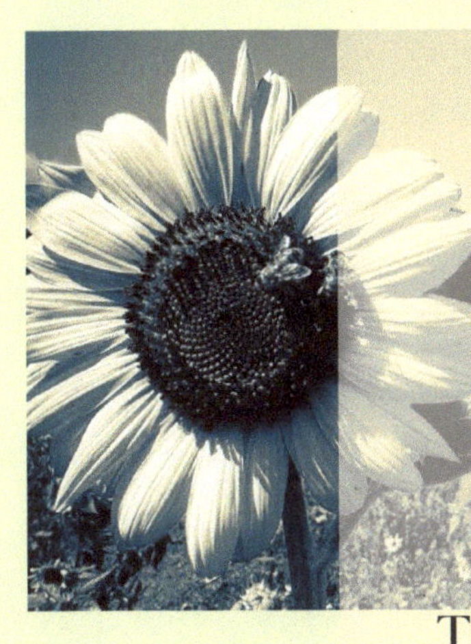

The snips mist
A level cut
The lesson missed
The withered gut
The old that dust
The poison well
Of the petals that fell

The ebb it sways to better days
The flow it says to let it go
To hang the pendulum give and takes
It's control feels way below
World of the dew so far and few
Who but you that caught the view
Of the petals that fell

The give and take
The heart and ache
The stem and vase
A forgotten slate
A given state
The present of the flowers tell
Of the petals that fell

-CI'24

Photo by : Lexi Re'

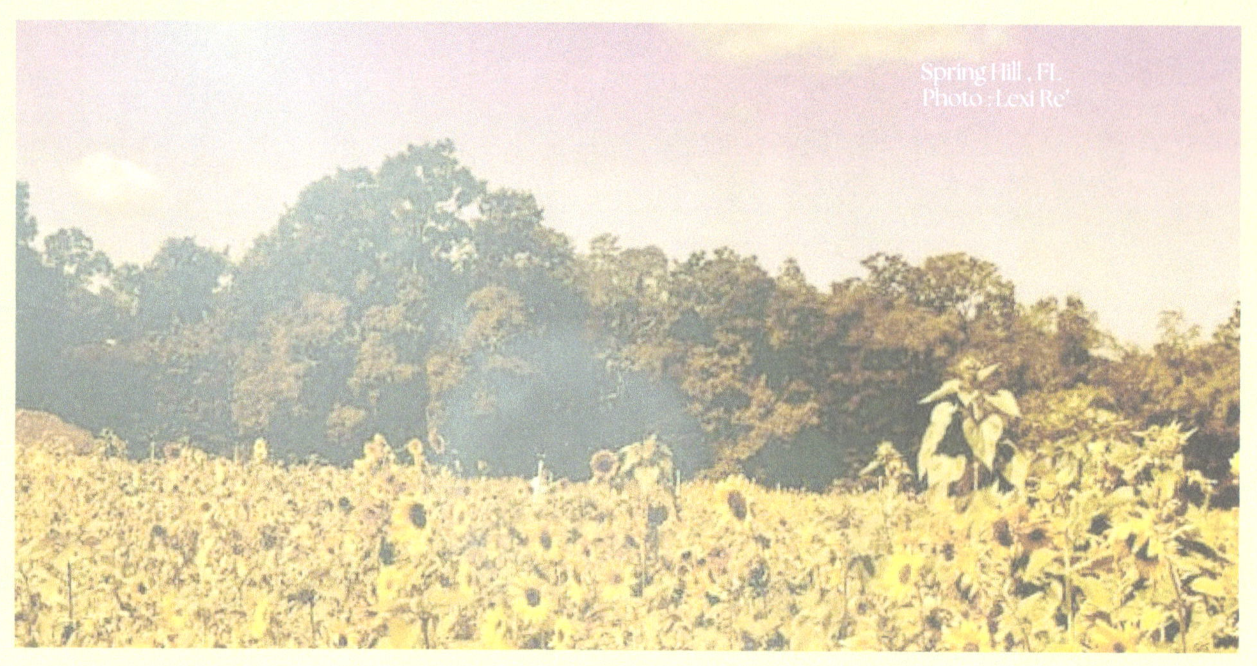

It was morning when sat in meditation in looking at the rose bush. I could see the thousand eyes of the dew looking back at me. I sat and thought who I was to each dew that reflected back to me. That being the last thought to recede, I just was. I was the looker and the looked at. We melded together and took a breath together then. The petals fell , and I was the only one to see it. That moment was just for me.

I like to consider time as a faculty of moments. One moment after the next. Time as far as an instinctive comfort was something I always struggled with. What day it was , losing track of time, and remembering many vivid dreams. These are all things that I have been trying to master within my depths. Being self-educated from my years of private study , years of therapeutic experiment , and sometimes radical means of understanding.

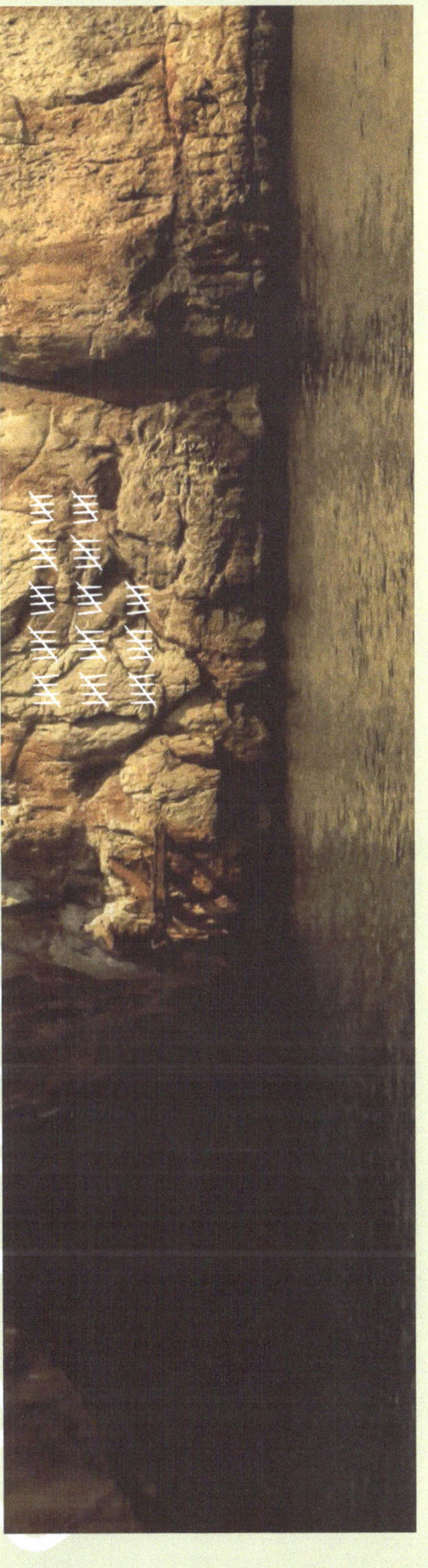

Time in itself is confusing to me. The origins , "business" hours, and birthday times. Seasons we could obviously tell visually but don't have this certain memorial timestamp for sections of memories. "T'was autumn at dusk for supper" is a fun way to look at it for me. All of them have specific time associations and categorizations. All are still of the same faculty of moments. If there are two childbirths across the globe from each other , in the same moment both babies arrived , but different times. So for baby number 1 was born on a different day, time , week or even month. Just by mental parameters time is all segregated into so many different ways. Still the same moment!

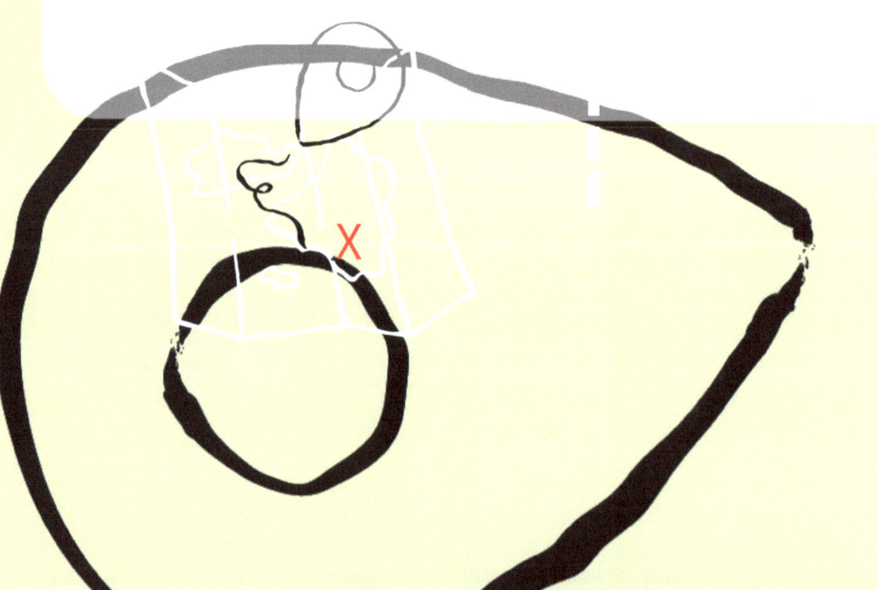

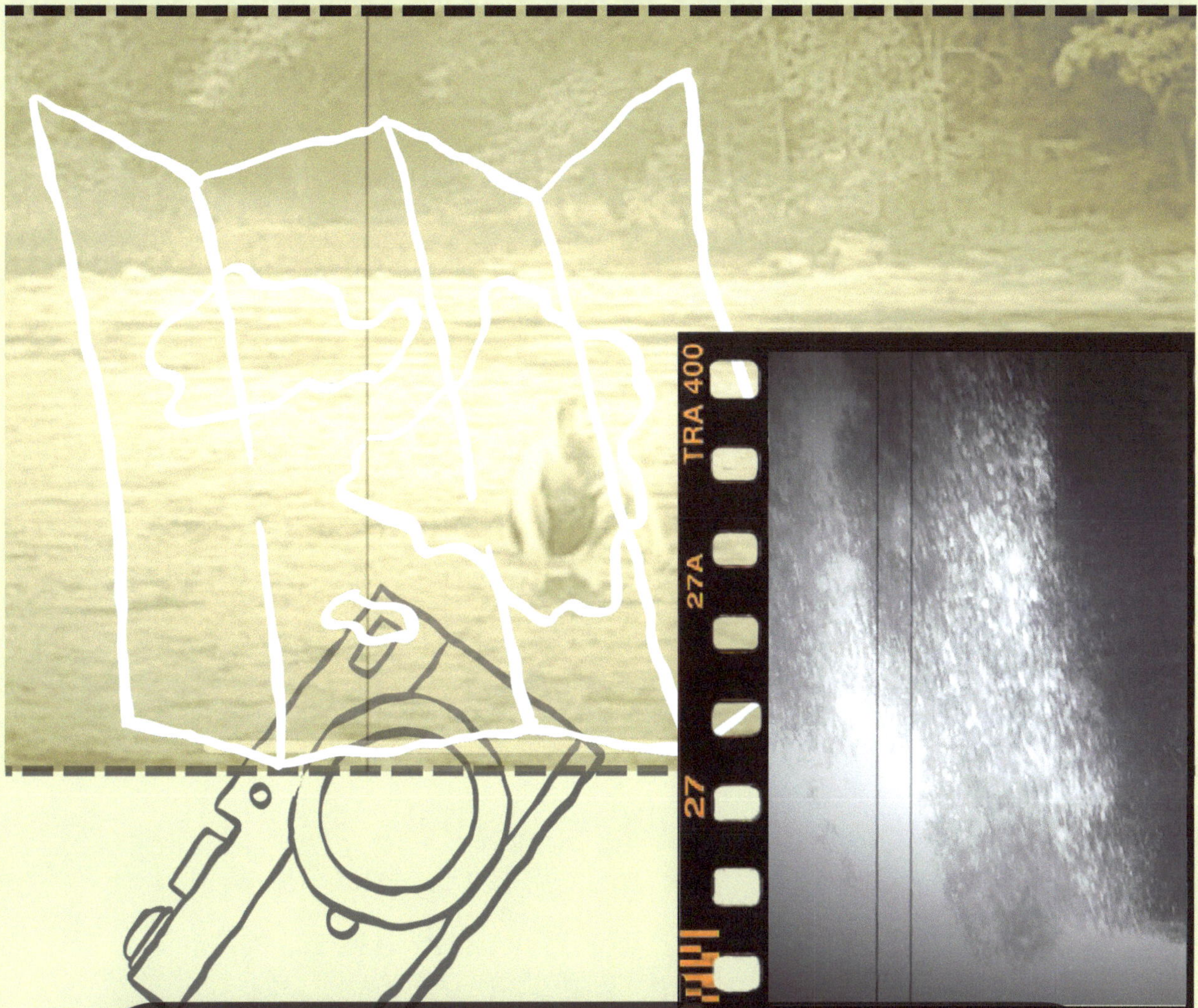

Being on the road is one of those instances where it could seem like its taking forever or kind of zone out and blink to fast you pass an exit we meant to get off at. The open road has its blessings for sure but can be one of the most stressful aspects of everyday life. Being on 4 separate road trips across 30 plus states I've learned how important stopping to take fun breaks instead of just stretching my legs.

Beach times

The Beach is so medicinal for me and a lot of others. A perfect combination of the salt, breeze, and sounds of the shore that make it so magical for some. Its so much fun and the time could fly by and seem like it has gone by so fast and before you know it the sun is setting.

Venice FL

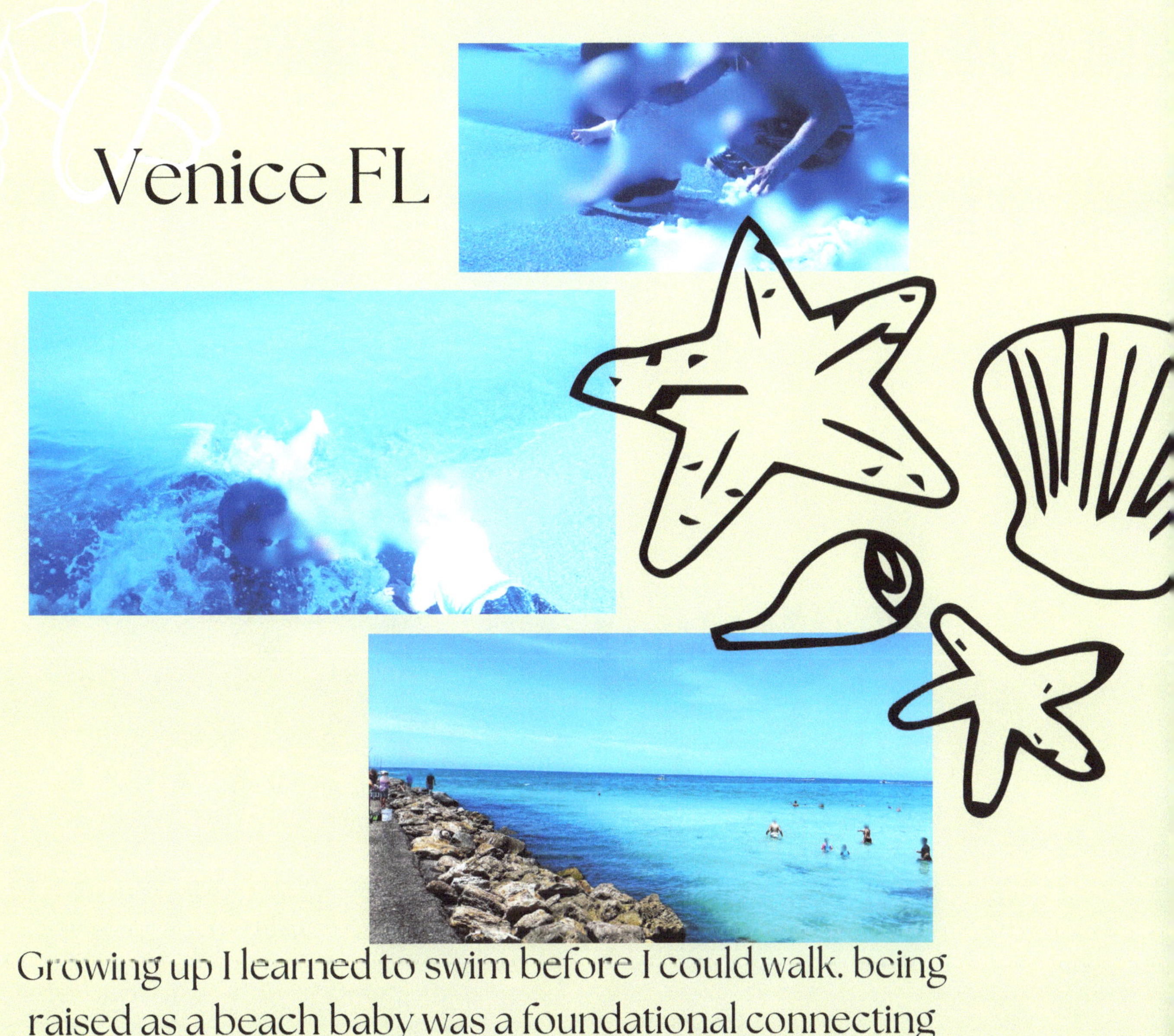

Growing up I learned to swim before I could walk. being raised as a beach baby was a foundational connecting and emotional experience every time.
Raising kids here is also has been a great bonding experience with all family members whether it be reunions or just for the Sunday picnic .

the need for the beach

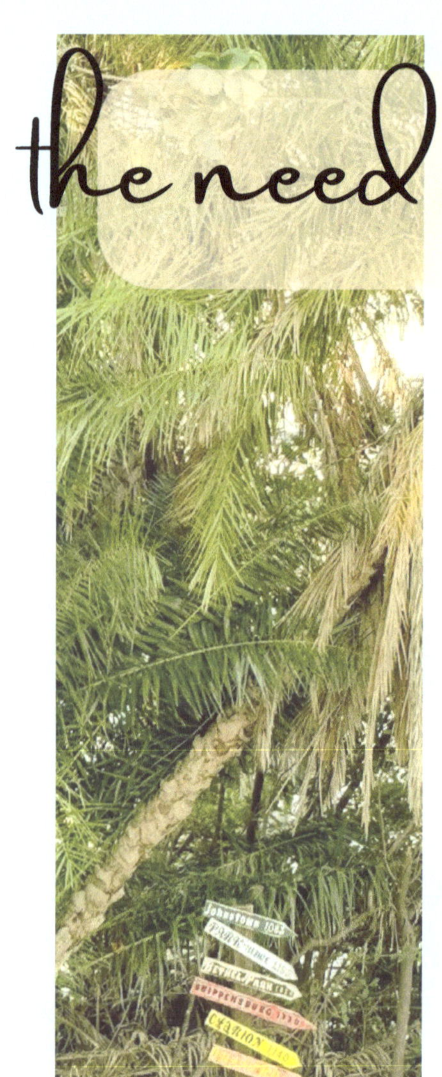

We usually have unilateral thoughts when we get to the beach. I have been to so many beaches and spent so much time at them meditating that it has allowed me to have some "higher forms of thought" about them.

For one , some natural beaches are ancient. That for every grain of sand we step on is a star in the sky. That ever grain when you look so close , has its own world.

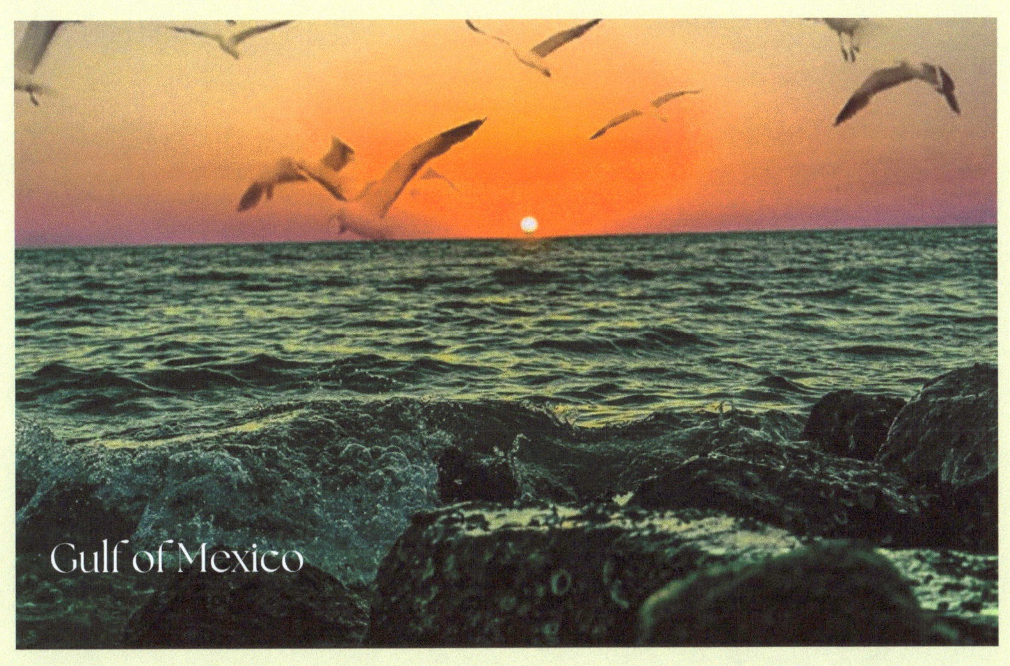

There are always ways to find peace on the beach. Locally we have free morning yoga classes, drum circles , national sandcastle competition, and some of the best ranked beaches in the world.

The sand is a part of what makes a really nice beach for me. Not only is it grounding but it makes for an easier jog or chasing your children around.

Some of the beaches are more " man- made" and have special sand brought in . Siesta Key Beach in Sarasota Florida has pristine crushed quartz sand !

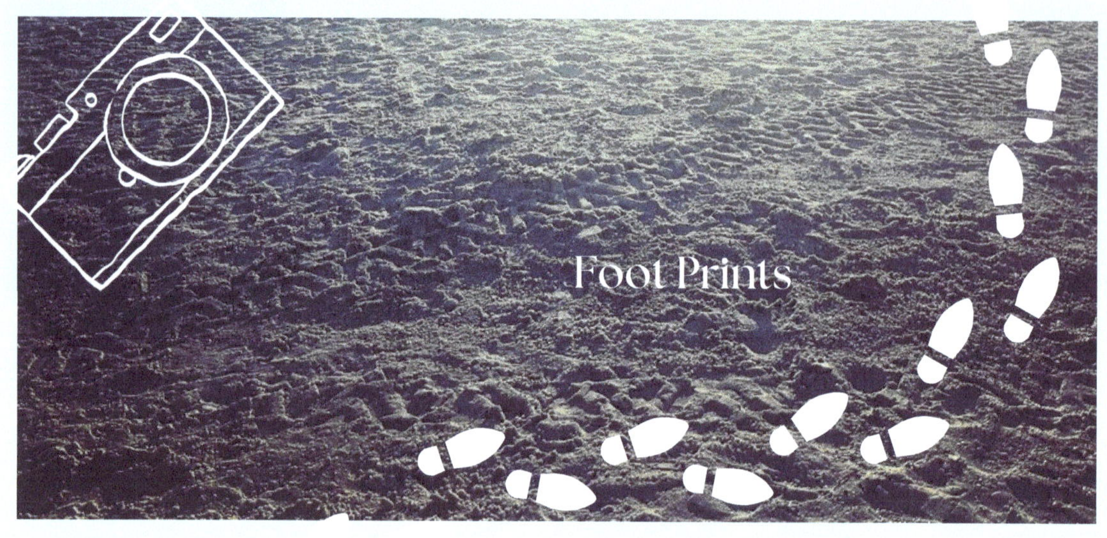

Foot Prints

he cupped the sand
of the weight of his foot
frantically poured in a hour
that's sands the glass forged from
sand to count the sun
and the moon
to save his foot print in time
before it was taken by the tide

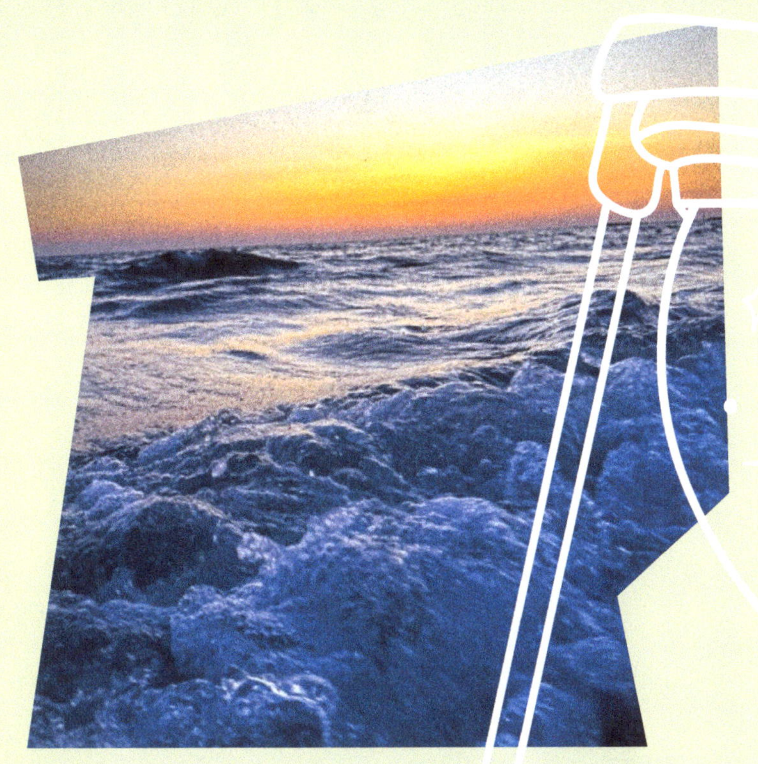

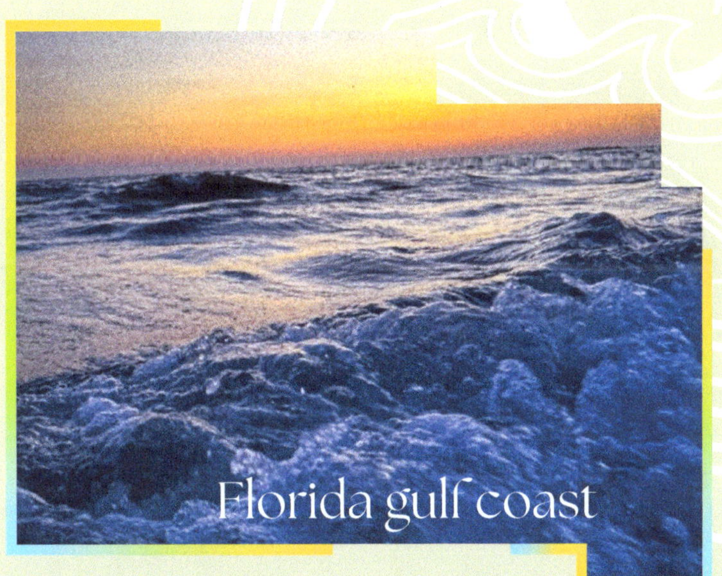

Florida gulf coast

Im blessed by you being
a sight for you seeing
me looking into your eyes
Our souls did first kiss
a Betrothal of bliss
temporally stamped in mind.

The sunset is a romantic landmark.
Its a global daily destination.
High prices to eat , live and work that can see sunset is actually priceless. The romantic loving experience of a rooftop sunset dinner, is the same that can be had with a sandwich and a good conversation with my toes in the water.

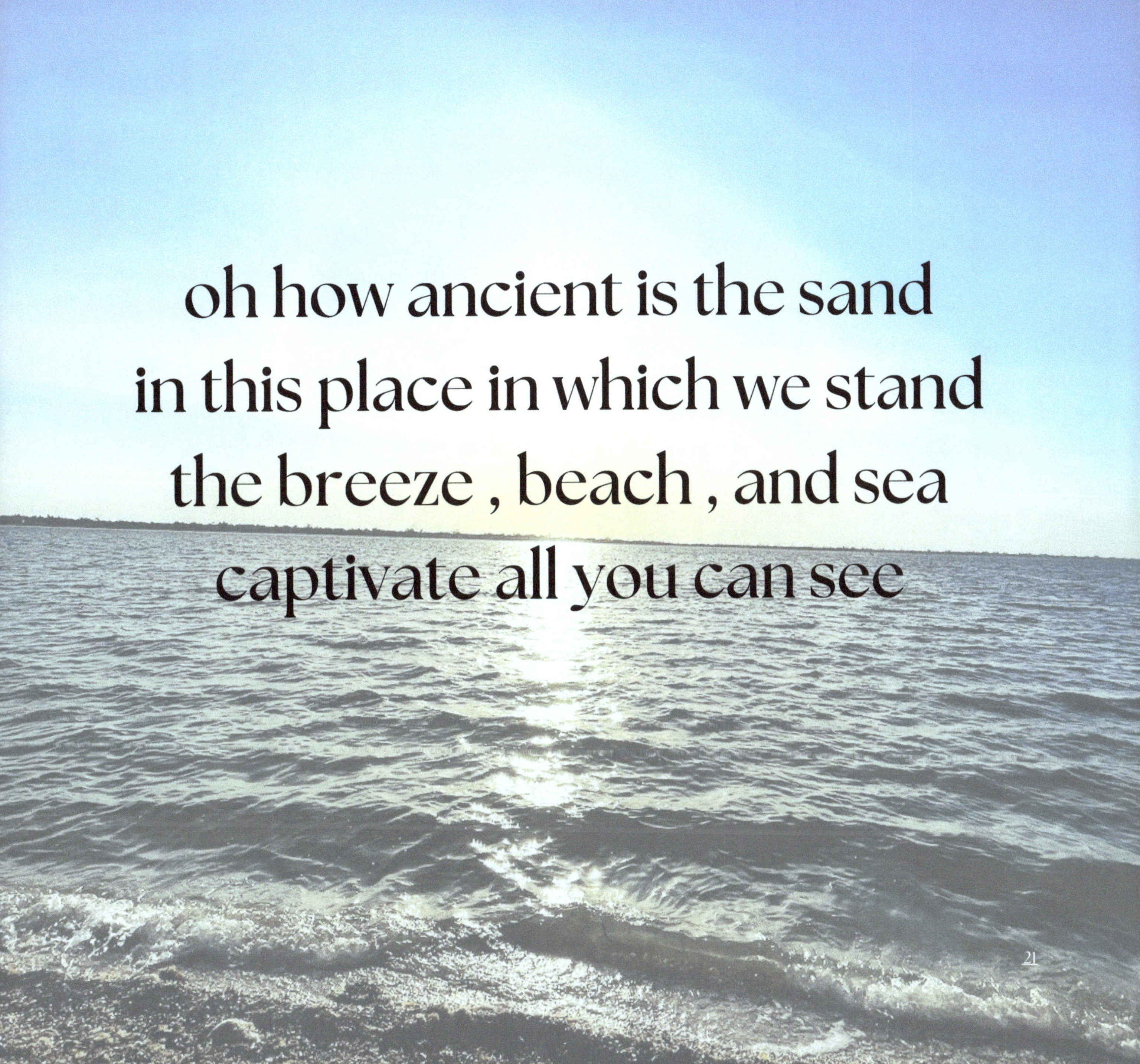

oh how ancient is the sand
in this place in which we stand
the breeze , beach , and sea
captivate all you can see

Dusk

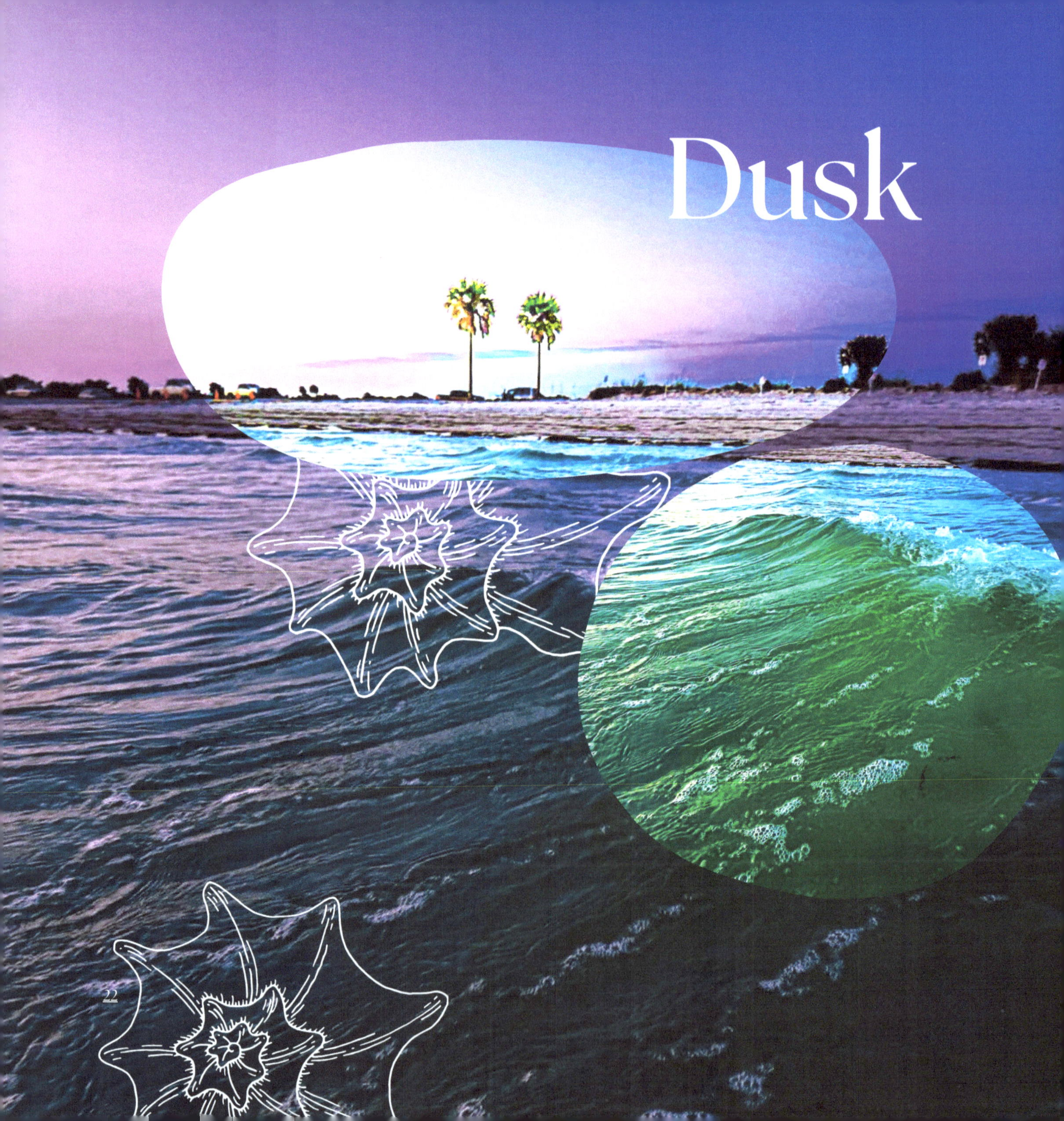

Blue Ridge Parkway ,North Carolina

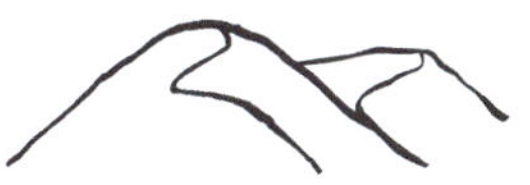

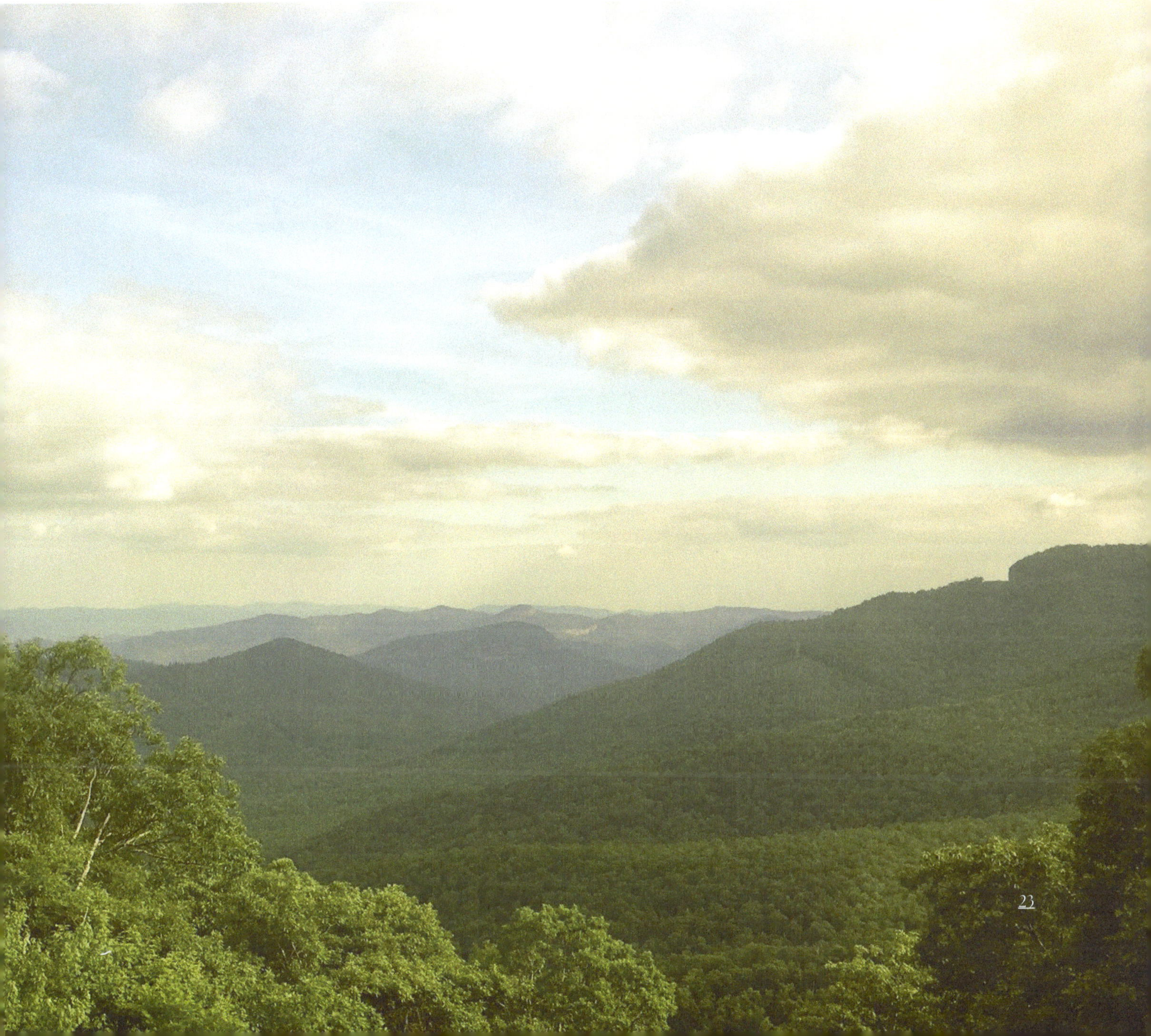

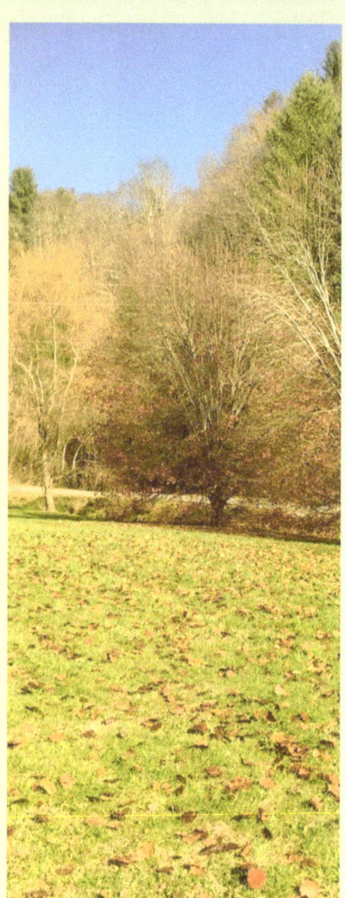
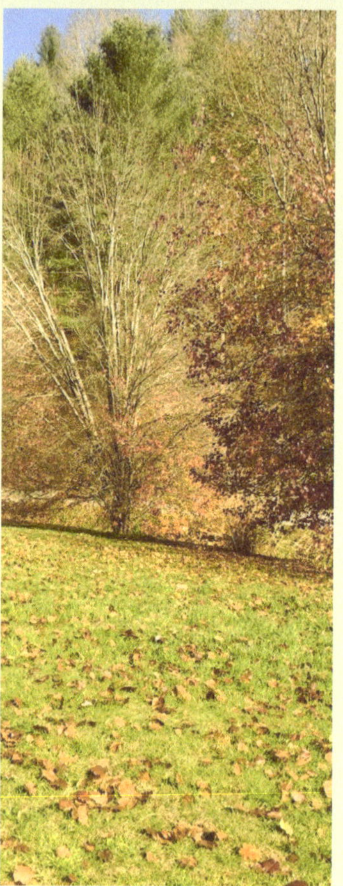
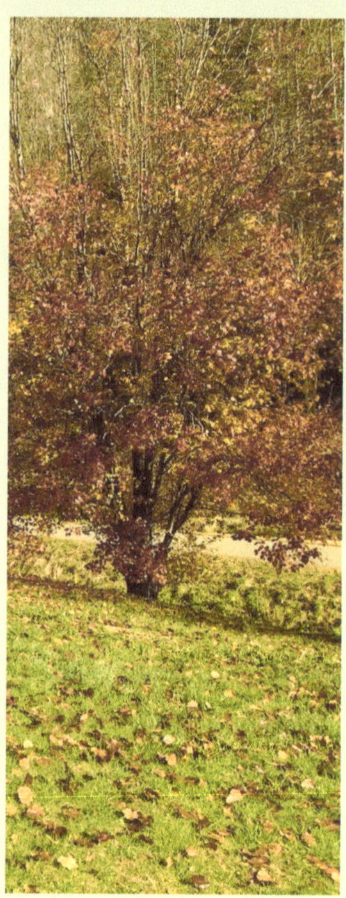

Blue Ridge Parkway , North Carolina

What a better synonym of time then the seasons. The constant change cycle every year with small amounts of growth each year. Its so helpful if we take in this aspect of life and apply it to our emotional and mental health. Part of the combination of the contents stones of the mountains literally and being on the mountain tops conquering goals of change .

Little Distortions

In Time

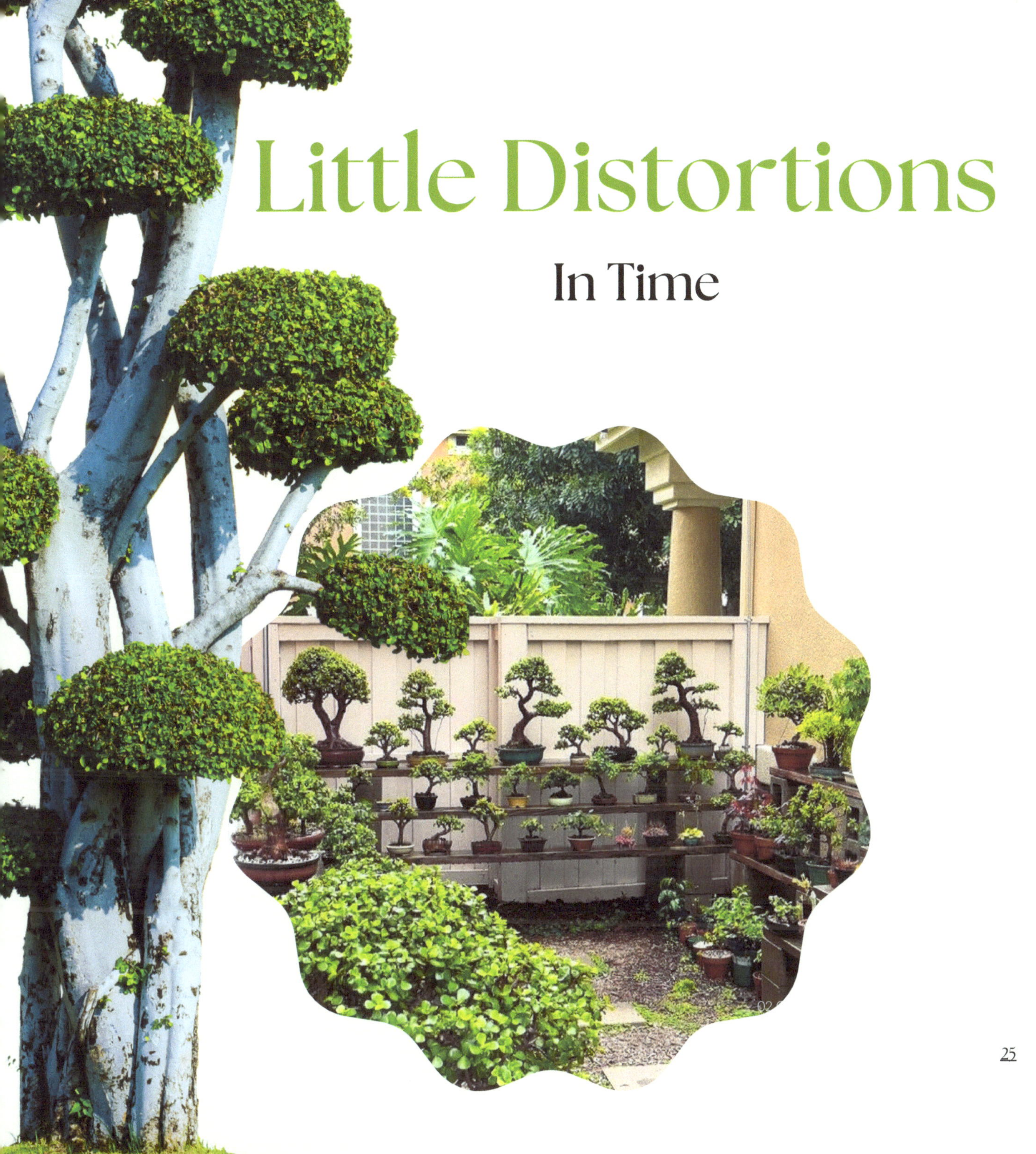

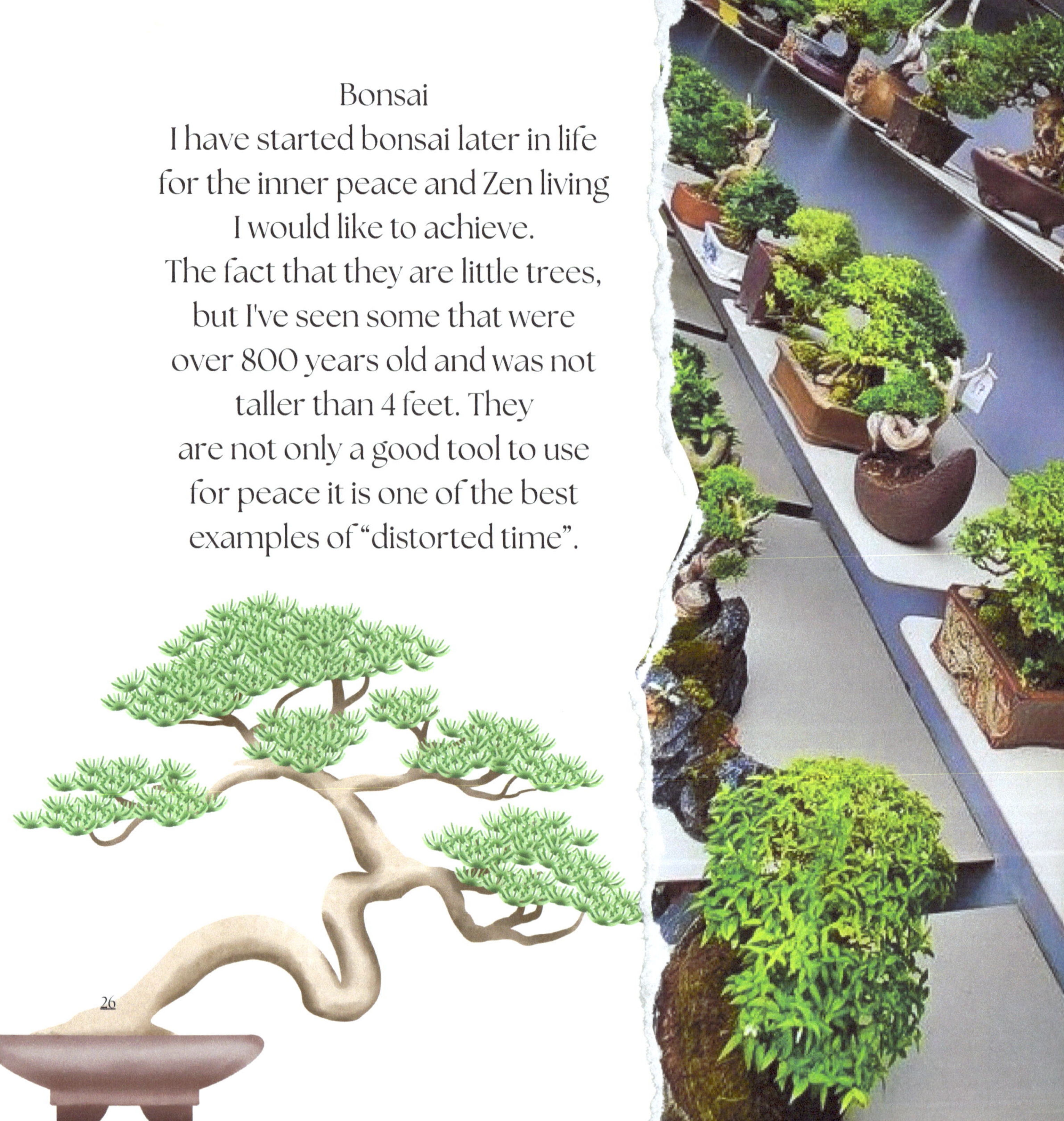

Bonsai

I have started bonsai later in life for the inner peace and Zen living I would like to achieve. The fact that they are little trees, but I've seen some that were over 800 years old and was not taller than 4 feet. They are not only a good tool to use for peace it is one of the best examples of "distorted time".

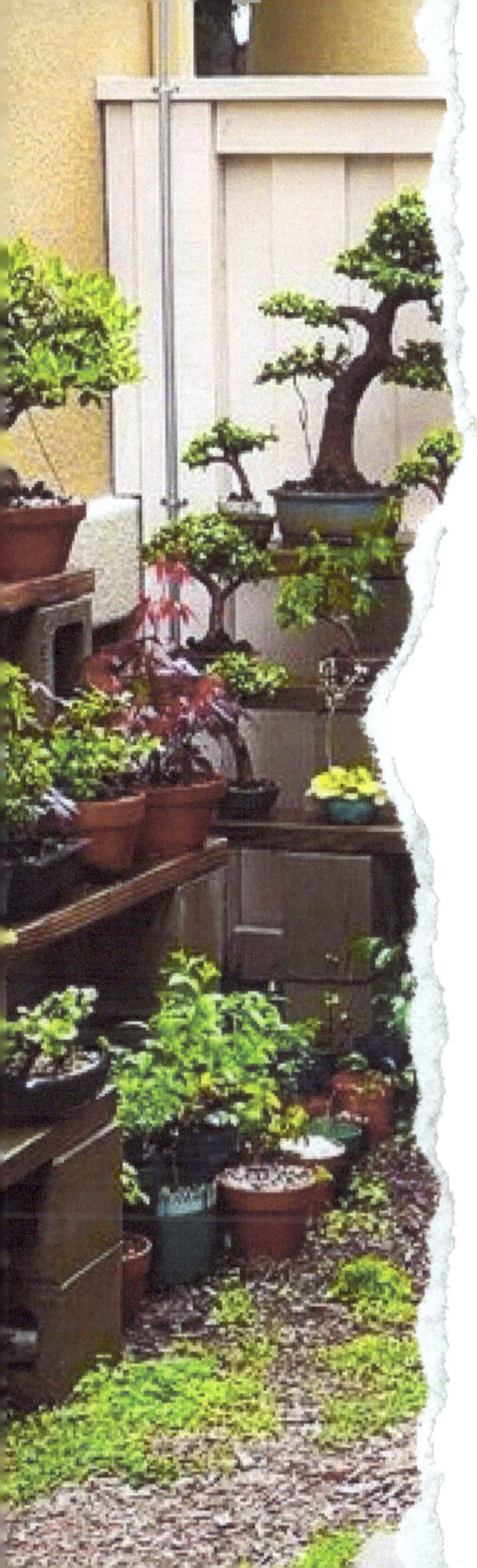

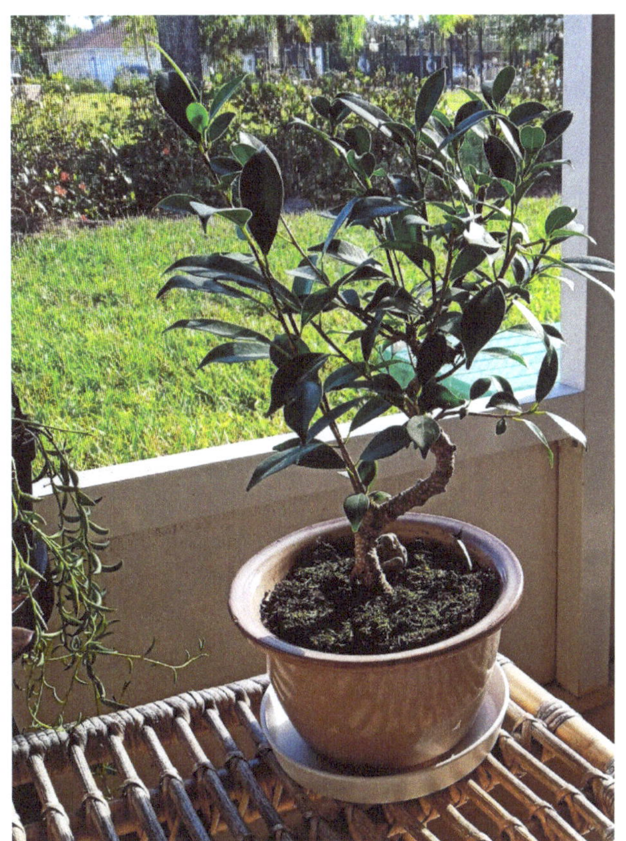

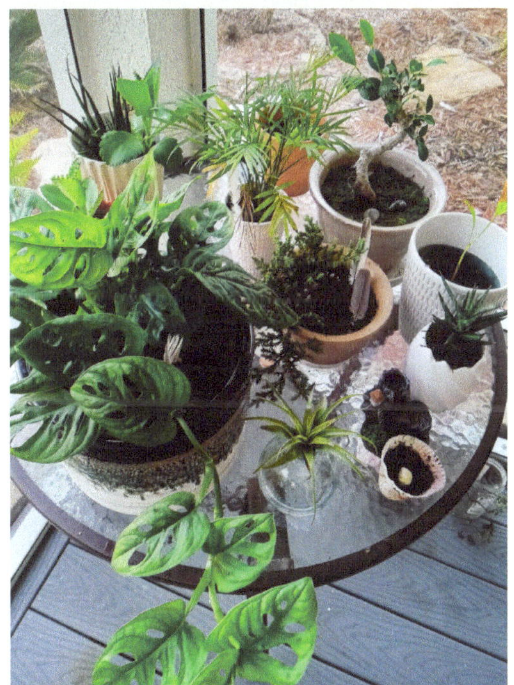

Planting and tending to plants is a very special way to be in the moment. If you are gardening for food , its this symbiosis where you take care of what takes care of you . Taking a moment to sit with the miracle of large amounts of food come from a tiny handful of seeds.

Take a moment to be grateful.

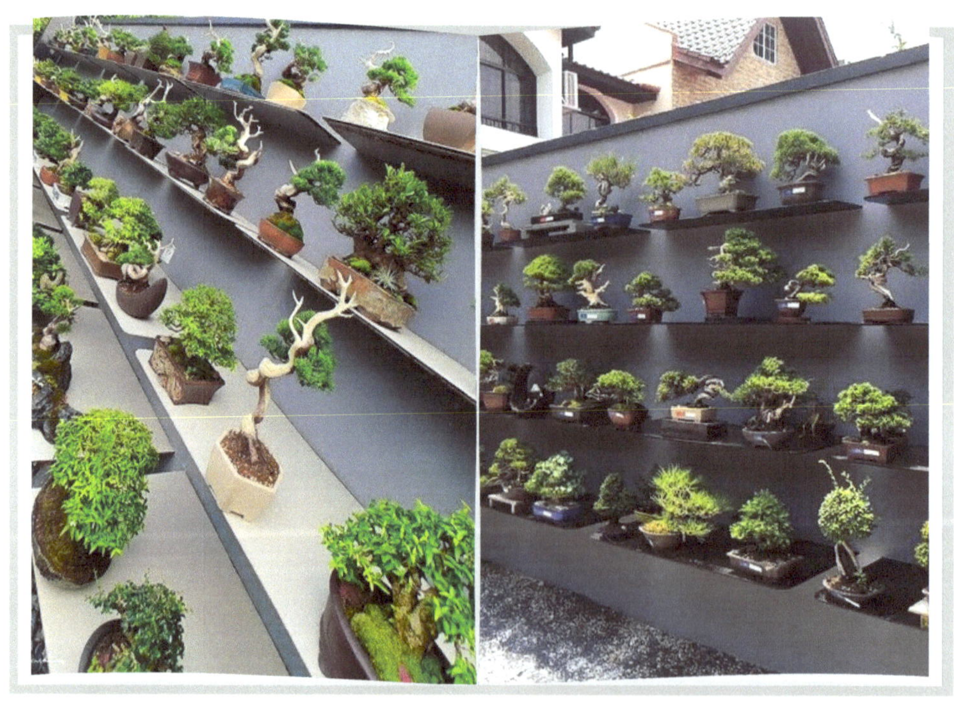

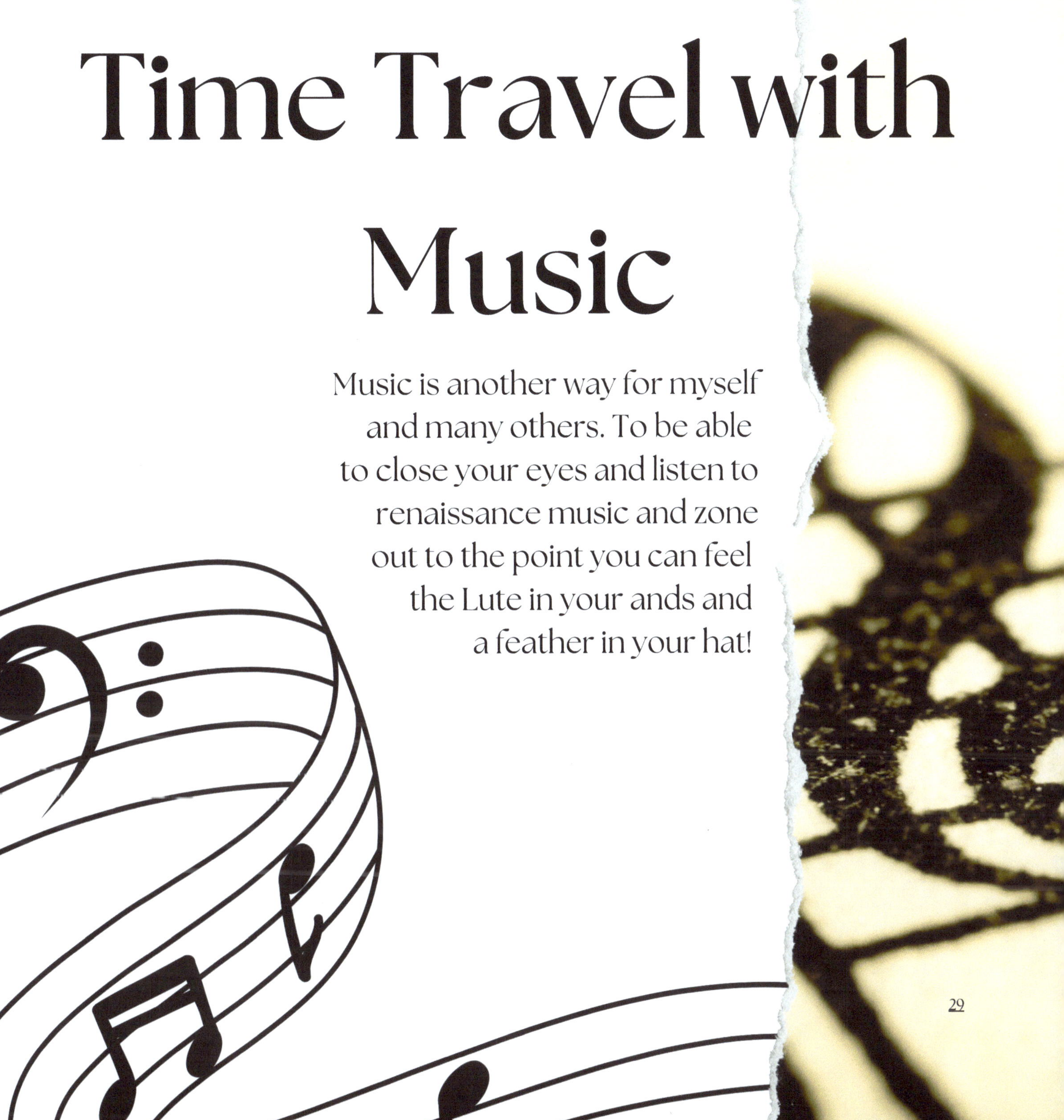

Time Travel with Music

Music is another way for myself and many others. To be able to close your eyes and listen to renaissance music and zone out to the point you can feel the Lute in your ands and a feather in your hat!

Music has been in my family for a long time. A long "Long" time. On one side of my family , maiden name Long , and the other side Steele. Both have vast musical lineage in the Bible Belt since the 1700's.

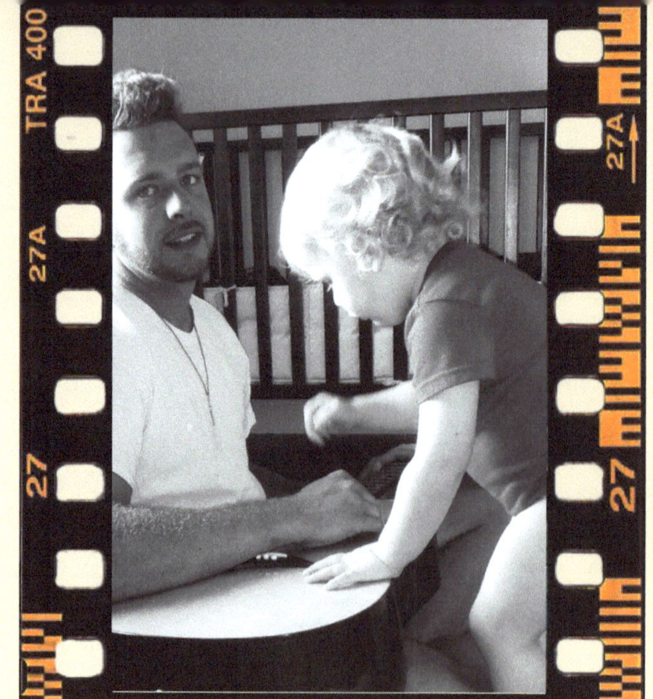

Music not only timestamps experiences and time periods but the ability to play is passed down through time. From generation to generation the genetic structure to play and the rhythm we end up being born with.

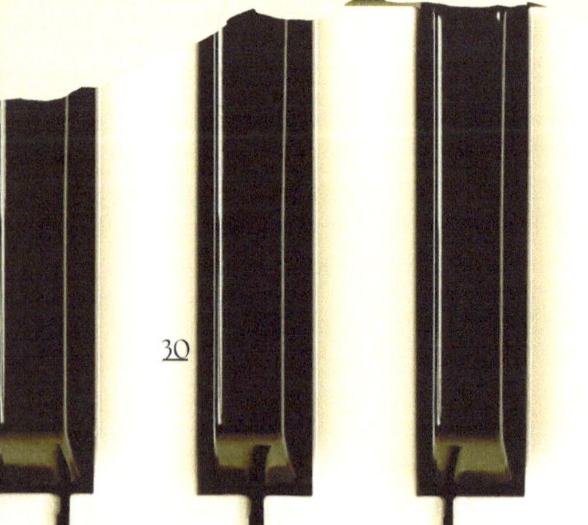
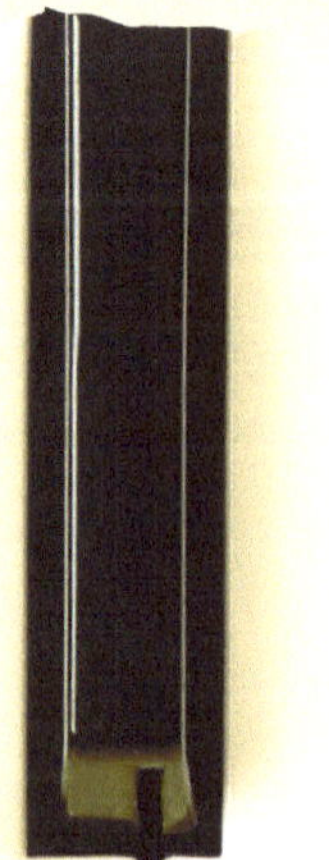
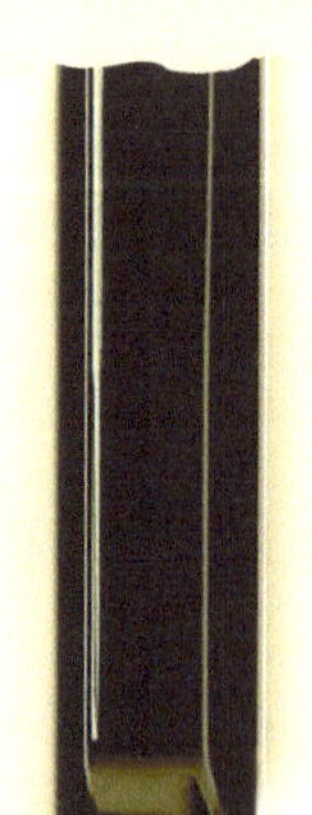
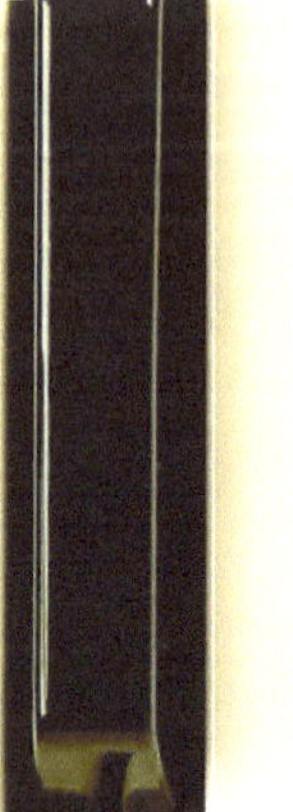

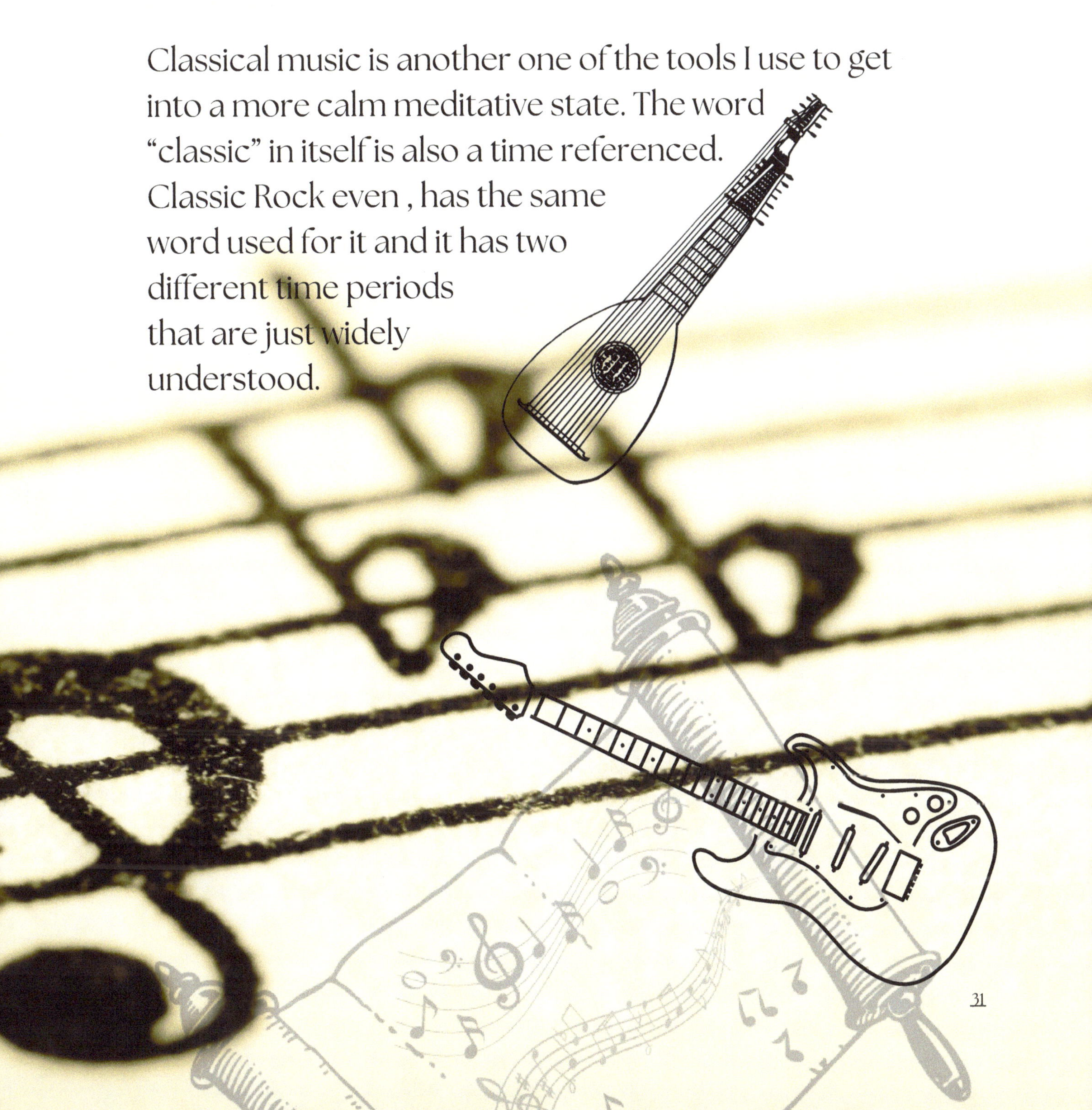

Classical music is another one of the tools I use to get into a more calm meditative state. The word "classic" in itself is also a time referenced. Classic Rock even , has the same word used for it and it has two different time periods that are just widely understood.

Lucid dreams is one of my favorite topics to study and practice. Its a place where time is irrelevant. You can time travel and not even blink an eye. You can do almost anything, any place, and anytime . It can be meditative , but it also can be extremely chaotic. Learning how to control lucid things in my dreams has been one of the not only most fun experience , it has had a lot of residual effects too. It has allowed me to heal from fears, conquer quests from a castle, or take off and fly like superman. If you never felt the confidence that when you can take off like a rocket any second you want, you need to. The dream space is unlike anything else.

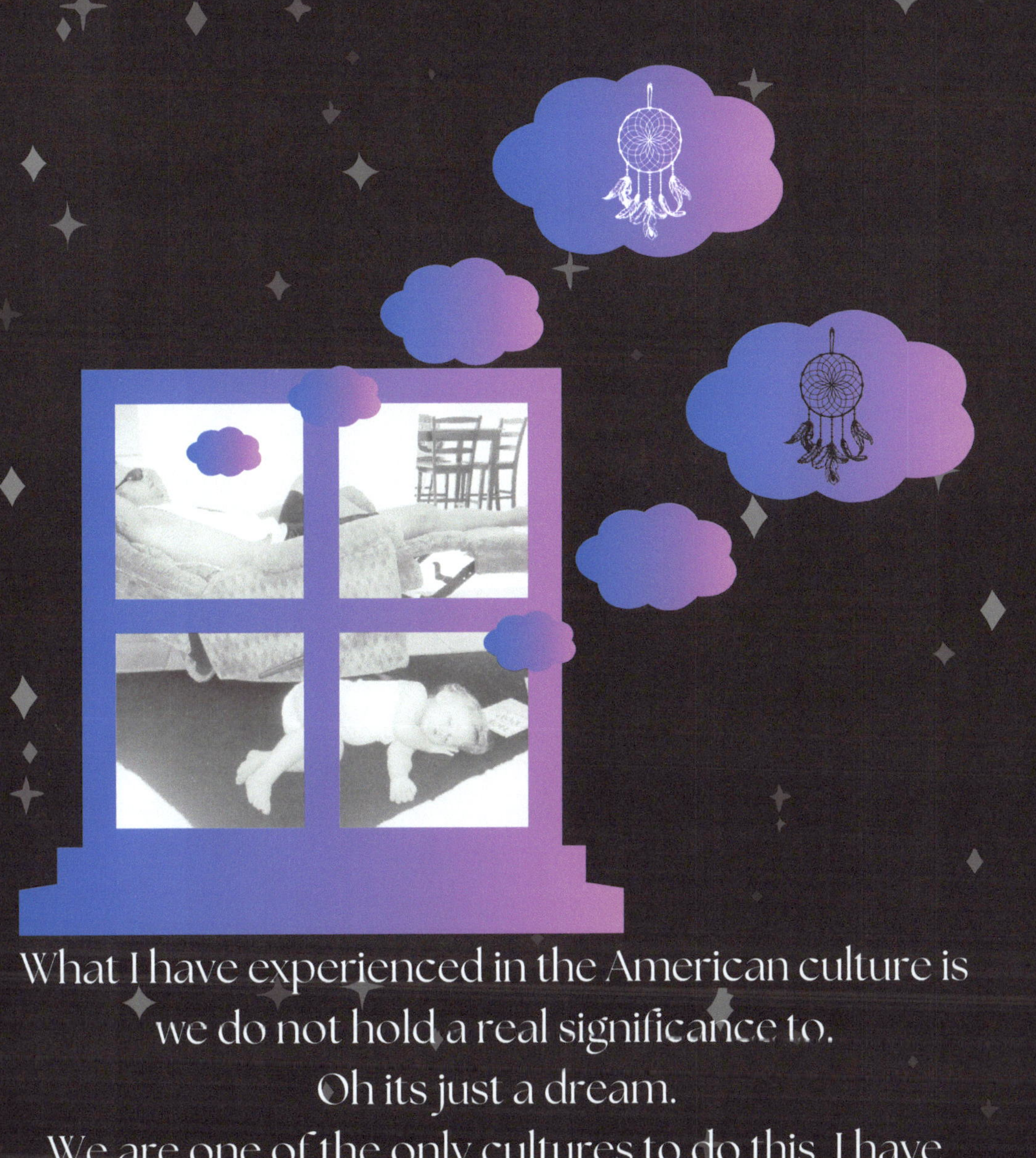

What I have experienced in the American culture is
we do not hold a real significance to.
Oh its just a dream.
We are one of the only cultures to do this. I have
one book and may other snippets of literature
coupled with countless videos of information
of how to basically be a lucid dream architect.

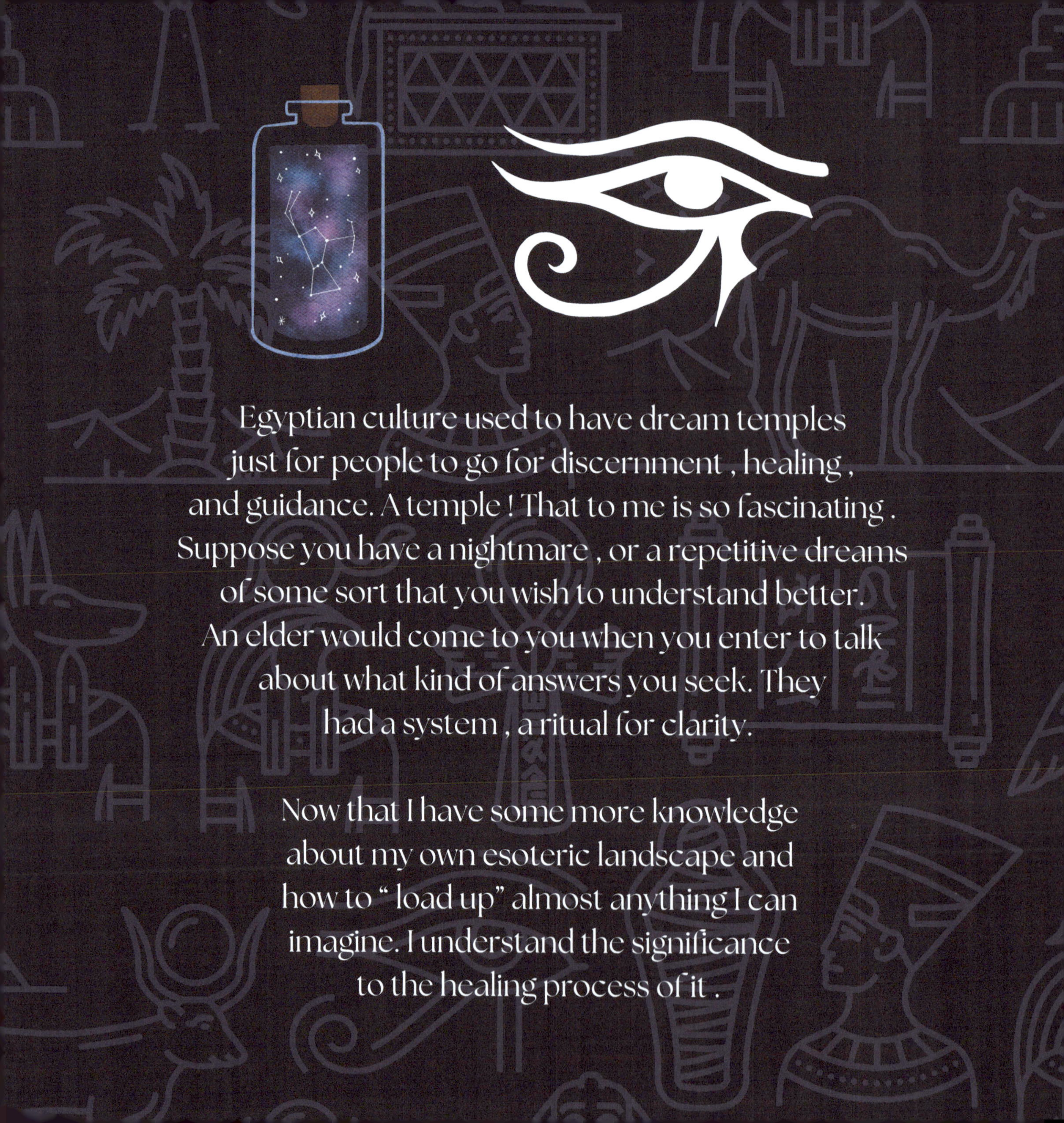

Egyptian culture used to have dream temples
just for people to go for discernment , healing ,
and guidance. A temple ! That to me is so fascinating .
Suppose you have a nightmare , or a repetitive dreams
of some sort that you wish to understand better.
An elder would come to you when you enter to talk
about what kind of answers you seek. They
had a system , a ritual for clarity.

Now that I have some more knowledge
about my own esoteric landscape and
how to " load up" almost anything I can
imagine. I understand the significance
to the healing process of it .

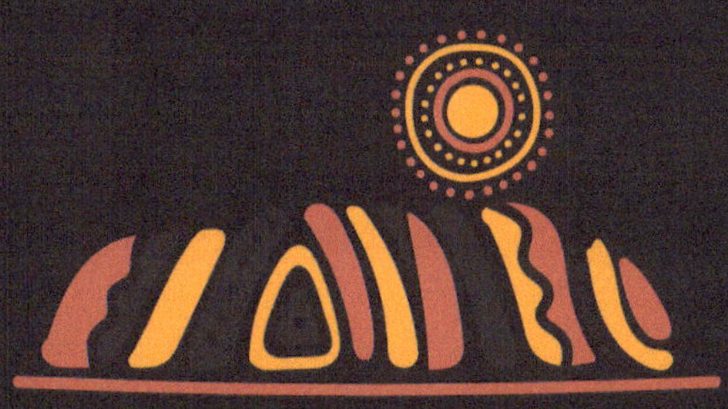

Aboriginals in Australia had so much finesse and precision about their lucid dreaming. It has helped actual communication of tribes across the country. In two different sections separated by what seems like countless miles, meet in their dreams. Discuss a location , what there bringing to trade or what the purpose of the meeting.

Then on that information alone, they would meet sometime 60 plus miles away in the middle of nowhere with nothing to indicate location other than the dream. They have been doing this for a very long time.

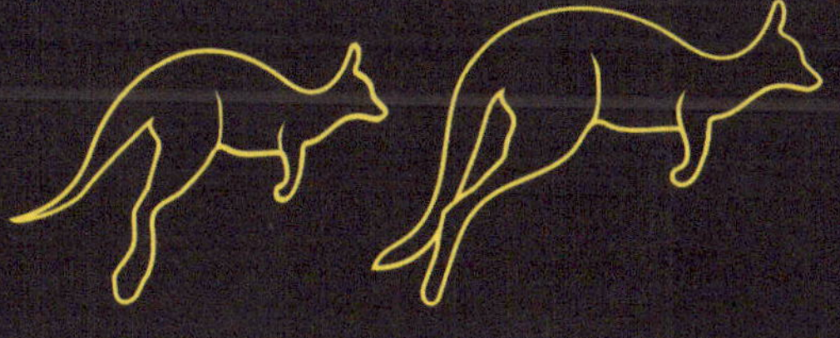

Native Americans made
dream catchers
so they would ward off evil
spitrits and over all
protection .

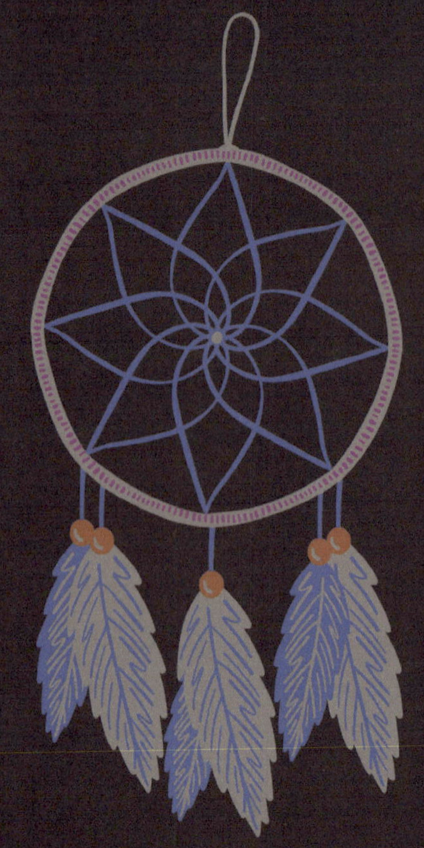

Even in the Christian bible. There was a man named Daniel could decipher dreams so well that he gave counsel to leaders and kings that were reguarded in high places.

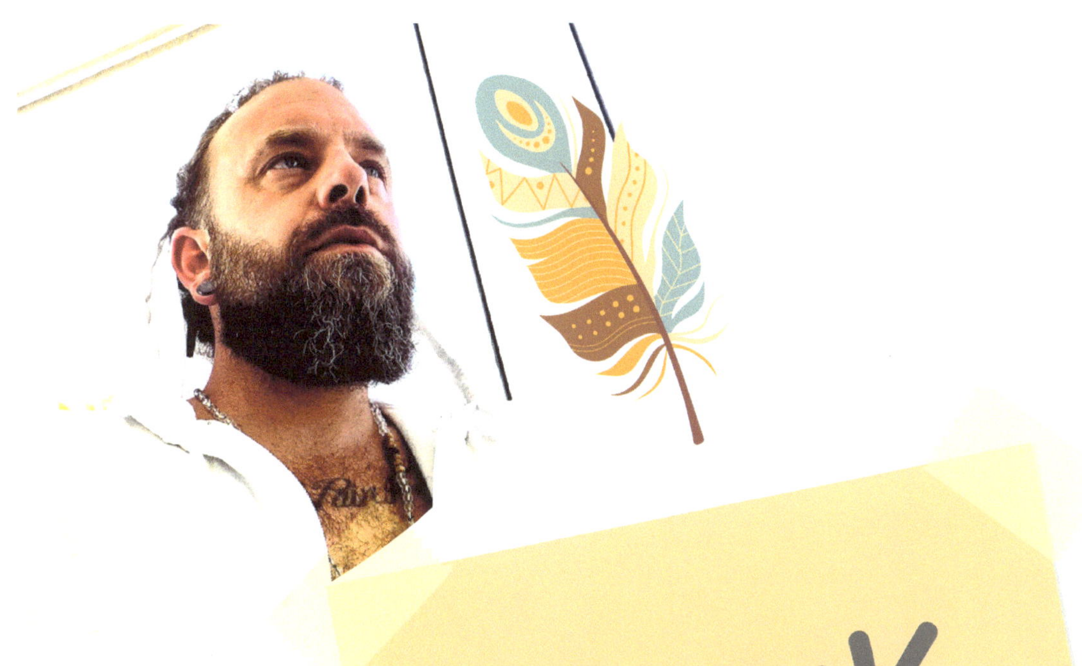

THANK YOU

There are many more neat aspects of time than we have the time for. We can peer through time to see how other practices , methodology and outlooks helped what we have formed today as Time.

I really appreciate the time it took to make this book I really appreciate your time and effort that went into purchase this book and the time it took to read it. Even if it takes one page at a time.

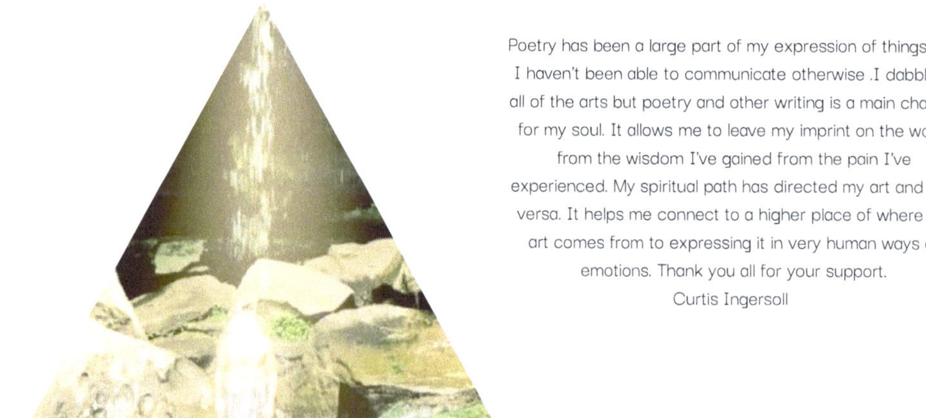

Poetry has been a large part of my expression of things that I haven't been able to communicate otherwise .I dabble in all of the arts but poetry and other writing is a main channel for my soul. It allows me to leave my imprint on the world from the wisdom I've gained from the pain I've experienced. My spiritual path has directed my art and visa versa. It helps me connect to a higher place of where my art comes from to expressing it in very human ways of emotions. Thank you all for your support.

Curtis Ingersoll

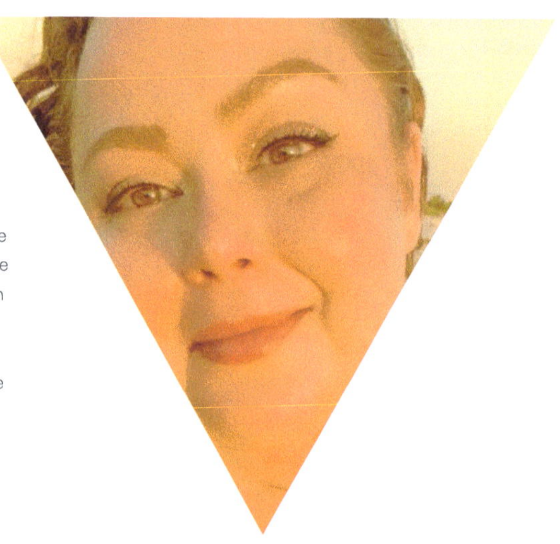

My passion for photography comes from nature. Capturing a moment of a bird singing in the breeze. The way the last bit of sun reflects the joy on a persons face in that moment. The way that the sun makes the ocean sparkle with magic. I take enjoyment in capturing old buildings with history. The way that walking through nature tells me stories about how things must die to be reborn. Life is beauty and I want to share that experience through my photos with the world.

Lexi Re'

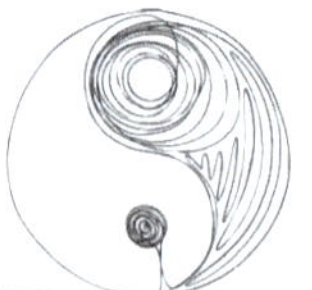

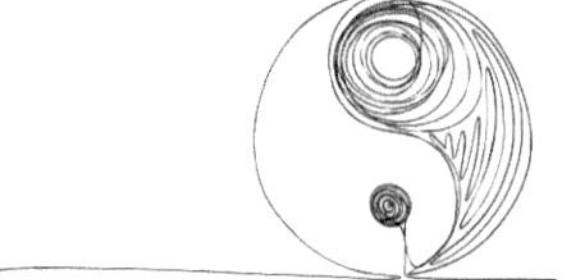

www.ingramcontent.com/pod-product-compliance
Lightning Source LLC
LaVergne TN
LVHW071202160826
845679LV00003B/722

* 9 7 9 8 8 9 5 6 9 1 3 8 0 *